THE ASSIGNMENT:

THE DREAM & THE DESTINY

VOLUME 1

by

MIKE MURDOCK

Unless otherwise indicated, all Scripture quotations are taken from the King James Version of the Bible.

The Assignment: The Dream & The Destiny,
Volume 1
Copyright © 1996 by Mike Murdock
ISBN 1-56394-053-1

Published by Wisdom International
P. O. Box 99 • Denton, Texas 76202

TABLE OF CONTENTS

━━━━━➤●◄━━━━━

~ 1 ~

EVERYTHING GOD CREATED WAS CREATED TO SOLVE A PROBLEM.

Creativity is the search for solutions.

Let me illustrate. In large gatherings of the past, speakers could not be heard clearly. So, microphones and public address systems were created. Eyeglasses were created for those who have difficulty seeing.

Problems are the catalysts for *creativity*. When an inventor—whether it is Thomas Edison or whomever—invents something, his creativity is based on an existing problem. He *solves* the problem, and he is *rewarded* accordingly.

Why did you buy your car? Because it solved a transportation problem. Why do you watch the news each evening on television? It solves an information problem.

Mechanics solve *car* problems.
Dentists solve *tooth* problems.
Lawyers solve *legal* problems.
Mothers solve *emotional* problems.
Accountants solve *tax* problems.

That is why God created us. God wanted a *love* relationship. He wanted to be *chosen, pursued,* and *treasured.* So, He created Adam and Eve.

But Adam had a problem: He needed *human* companionship. "And the Lord God said, It is not good that the man should be alone; I will make him an help meet for him. And the Lord God caused a deep sleep to fall upon Adam, and he slept: and he took one of his ribs, and closed up the flesh instead thereof; And the rib, which the Lord God had taken from man, made he a woman, and brought her unto the man. And Adam said, This is now bone of my bones, and flesh of my flesh: she shall be called Woman, because she was taken out of Man" (Genesis 2:18,21-23). You see, each one of us is a *solution.*

So, when you open your eyes every morning, you are looking into an entire world *crammed* with *solutions.* Everything created is a solution...to somebody, somewhere, at some time.

You are a solution to somebody.

This means you are a reward to someone. Somebody *needs* you. Somebody *wants* you. You are *necessary* to somebody, somewhere...*today*

Read these powerful words: "Then the word of the Lord came unto me, saying, Before I formed thee in the belly I knew thee; and before thou camest forth out of the womb I sanctified thee, and I ordained thee a prophet unto the nations" (Jeremiah 1:4,5).

You were created for a specific and very special purpose...*to solve a specific problem on earth.* I call this, *The Assignment.*

God is not a respecter of persons. He created Jeremiah for a special time and season and for a special people. It is the same with you.

God will assist you in *your Assignment*. "For thou shalt go to all that I shall send thee, and whatsoever I command thee thou shalt speak. Be not afraid of their faces: for I am with thee to deliver thee, saith the Lord" (Jeremiah 1:7,8).

So God created Eve to solve a problem for Adam. Then they both had a problem! Who would take care of them in their old age? So, God gave them *children*. "Lo, children are an heritage of the Lord: and the fruit of the womb is his reward. As arrows are in the hand of a mighty man; so are children of the youth. Happy is the man that hath his quiver full of them: they shall not be ashamed, but they shall speak with the enemies in the gate" (Psalm 127:3-5).

You see, *the wife is a solution to her husband.* "Thy wife shall be as a fruitful vine by the sides of thine house: thy children like olive plants round about thy table. Behold, that thus shall the man be blessed that feareth the Lord" (Psalm 128:3,4).

It is essential that you discover your Assignment and give yourself totally to it. "Let every man abide in the same calling wherein he was called" (1 Corinthians 7:20).

So, every *part* of you has an *Assignment*, a problem to solve. Your eyes have the Assignment of *seeing*. Your ears solve the problem of *hearing*.

Your eyes *see*.
Your ears *hear*.
Your hands *reach*.
Your feet *walk*.
Your mouth *speaks*.

Your nose *smells*.

So, everything in creation brings pleasure to God. "Thou art worthy, O Lord, to receive glory and honour and power: for Thou hast created all things, and for Thy pleasure they are and were created" (Revelation 4:11).

You see, everything God creates has a specific purpose. It solves a problem.

Your Assignment is to solve problems for those to whom you are sent.

❧ 2 ❧

You Are A Reward To Someone.

Somebody needs you.

Moses was needed as a leader to the children of Israel. He was their *reward*.

David was needed by the Israelites to defeat Goliath. He was a *reward* to King Saul as well, when he defeated Goliath and routed the Philistines.

Naomi needed a caretaker. Ruth was a reward for her, and so loyal that her devotion was recorded in the Scriptures for people to read of throughout generations.

The Jews would have been destroyed except for Esther. Esther was their answer, their solution, their *reward*.

Pharaoh desperately needed someone to interpret his dream. Joseph was a *reward* to him and subsequently to the people of Egypt.

Famine would have destroyed the Egyptians. Joseph was *their* reward because he interpreted the message from God through the dream of Pharaoh.

You see, everything God created is a *reward* to somebody.

Think about this. It is very important that you grasp *your* significance and value.

Your *patience* is a reward for somebody that others would not tolerate. Your *words* will motivate someone incapable of seeing what you see. It may be the mental, emotional, or spiritual qualities God has developed within you, *but somebody desperately needs you today.*

God planned you. Nobody else can be like you. *Nobody else* can do what you do. You are unlike anyone else on earth. Grasp this. Embrace it. God is not a duplicator. He is a Creator. You are absolutely perfect and genetically accurate for *solving a specific problem* for somebody on earth.

Somebody needs exactly *what you have been given* by God. Somebody is hungry and thirsty for *your* presence. Somebody will starve *without you* entering their life. Someone is literally dying, emotionally, mentally, or spiritually, *waiting for you* to come along and rescue them. Somebody has been lying awake at night praying that God would send you into their life.

You are their reward.

Now, it is important that you recognize that some people do not really need you. You are *not* their answer. You are *not* their solution. Do not take offense at this. God has somebody else planned for them.

You are not needed *everywhere*. You are only needed at a specific *place,* at a specific *time* and for a specific *person*.

Now, this person (or people) *qualifies* for your entrance into their life. They may not initially see you as being their reward, but you really are. You are *exactly* what God has ordered for their life.

Meditate on this truth. *Taste* it. *Feel* it.

There Are Three Important Keys To Remember Here:

1. *God Has Qualified You To Be A Perfect Solution To Someone.*

2. *It Is The Responsibility Of Others To Discern Your Assignment To Them.* The Pharisees did not discern that Jesus was assigned to them, but Zacchaeus did, and the relationship was born. Even Pharaoh of Egypt, an unbeliever, discerned that Joseph was the answer to his dream and dilemma. Thousands were sick and blind, but one cried out, "Jesus, Thou Son of David, have mercy on me." (See Mark 10:47.)

3. *When You Discover To Whom You Have Been Assigned, You Will Experience Great Peace, Fulfillment, And Provision For Your Own Life.*

You must determine and know well the anointing and calling on your own life. Stand strong, and stay linked to the Holy Spirit in total dependency, and God will direct you.

Look for opportunities to heal, strengthen, and bless others. Do good every time it is possible. "Withhold not good from them to whom it is due, when it is in the power of thine hand to do it" (Proverbs 3:27).

You are truly a gift and reward to those *to whom you are assigned.*

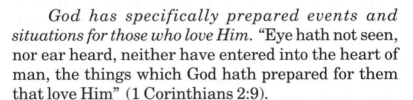

~ 3 ~

YOUR ASSIGNMENT IS NOT YOUR DECISION, BUT YOUR DISCOVERY.

God has specifically prepared events and situations for those who love Him. "Eye hath not seen, nor ear heard, neither have entered into the heart of man, the things which God hath prepared for them that love Him" (1 Corinthians 2:9).

You will only discern or discover those things, events, and your Assignment by the Holy Spirit. "But God hath revealed them unto us by His Spirit: for the Spirit searcheth all things, yea, the deep things of God" (1 Corinthians 2:10).

You must have the mind of Christ to discern your Assignment. "For who hath known the mind of the Lord, that He may instruct him? But we have the mind of Christ" (1 Corinthians 2:16).

Your gifts and skills were given to you by the Holy Spirit. "Now there are diversities of gifts, but the same Spirit. But all these worketh that one and the selfsame Spirit, dividing to every man severally as He will" (1 Corinthians 12:4,11).

Your gifts and skills are different from others around you. "Having then gifts differing according to the grace that is given to us, whether prophecy, let us prophesy according to the proportion of faith" (Romans 12:6).

Your gifts are from the Holy Spirit, the Comforter, Who walks beside you. "God also bearing them witness, both with signs and wonders, and with divers miracles, and gifts of the Holy Ghost, according to His own will?" (Hebrews 2:4).

You are sent by God into this generation. "...for thou shalt go to all that I shall send thee, and whatsoever I command thee thou shalt speak" (Jeremiah 1:7).

Your agenda has been predestined in the mind of God. "See, I have this day set thee over the nations and over the kingdoms, to root out, and to pull down, and to destroy, and to throw down, to build, and to plant" (Jeremiah 1:10).

God has a *plan.*

God has a plan for *your* life.

His plan for your life will require your obedience. "If ye be willing and obedient, ye shall eat the good of the land: But if ye refuse and rebel, ye shall be devoured with the sword: for the mouth of the Lord hath spoken it" (Isaiah 1:19,20).

His plan for your life will require a personal decision on your part to cooperate. "And it shall come to pass, if thou shalt hearken diligently unto the voice of the Lord thy God, to observe and to do all His commandments which I command thee this day, that the Lord thy God will set thee on high above all nations of the earth" (Deuteronomy 28:1).

His plan guarantees His blessing when completed. "And all these blessings shall come on thee, and overtake thee, if thou shalt hearken unto the voice of the Lord thy God. Blessed shall thou be in the city, and blessed shall thou be in the field" (Deuteronomy 28:2,3).

His plan gives life to you, while other plans will bring death. "I call heaven and earth to record this day against you, that I have set before you life and death, blessing and cursing: therefore choose life, that both thou and thy Seed may live" (Deuteronomy 30:19).

God decides *what* He *desires* for you to do.

You decide your obedience.

Predestination is the intention of God, not the decision of God. "The Lord is not slack concerning His promise, as some men count slackness; but is longsuffering to us-ward, not willing that any should perish, but that all should come to repentance" (2 Peter 3:9).

So we know that God does not want anyone to perish. *Yet, they do.* Daily. Millions have perished *without* Christ. So, even though you were predestined (intended by God) to be saved, it remains *your decision* to cooperate with Him and accept Him. "O Jerusalem, Jerusalem, thou that killest the prophets, and stonest them which are sent unto thee, how often would I have gathered thy children together, even as a hen gathereth her chickens under her wings, and ye would not! Behold, your house is left unto you desolate" (Matthew 23:37,38).

Think for a moment. Did the automobile instruct Henry Ford and declare to him what it had decided to be? Of course not. Mr. Ford named it. Did the airplane inform the Wright brothers that it was going to fly and be called an airplane? Of course not. Orville and Wilbur Wright declared it so.

The Creator *decides*.

The creation *discovers*.

The Creator decides what He has *intended* for you to become. The creation merely decides the degree of obedience and cooperation to *make* it so.

Products do not decide.

Manufacturers decide.

You are the product of God. He is the only One who can *reveal* the Assignment He decided for you at your birth.

∾ 4 ∾

What You Hate Is A Clue To Something You Are Assigned To Correct.

━━━━⫷●⫸━━━━

Anger is energy, power, and ability.

However, it requires *proper focus.* Have you ever wondered why others were not angry about situations that infuriated *you?* Of course you have. This is a clue to your Assignment.

Moses is an example. He hated slavery. When he saw an Egyptian beating an Israelite, fury arose. Why? Because he was a deliverer.

Remember These Three Wisdom Keys:

1. *You Cannot Correct What You Are Un-willing To Confront.*

2. *What You Permit Will Always Continue.*

3. *Behavior Permitted Is Behavior Perpetuated.*

I have a love for Wisdom. I have a hatred of ignorance. In my own life I have attended seminars where Scriptures were misquoted, truth was distorted, and error was dominant. It was almost impossible to sit and permit it.

You cannot really change or correct something unless you have a God-given hatred for it, whether it is sickness, injustice, racial prejudice, poverty, divorce, or abortion.

Many things are wrong in this country. But, they will never be changed until *someone is angry enough* about it to step forward and take charge.

For instance, abortion has subtly become accepted, although it is a truly devastating blight on the moral landscape of this country. It appears that no true and articulate spokesperson has yet emerged who is capable of turning the tide, although I thank God for those who are making significant efforts to do so!

The persuaded are persuasive.

Often I have asked God to give us someone with a burning desire who can *successfully* plead the case of the unborn child. I have asked God to provide a militant intellectual, passionate zealot who will link the Word of God with the gift of life in my generation—someone passionate and on fire.

That someone could be you.

I am not talking about the issue of bombing abortion clinics or murdering those who kill unborn children.

I am speaking of *an anointing*, a mantle, a calling—when someone *rises up* to complete their Assignment in this generation: to challenge, correct, and conquer the Seeds of rebellion that have grown up around us.

Your anger is important. Very important. Do not

ignore it. Satan dreads your fury. *An angry man is an awakened man.* An angry man changes the minds of others.

Focused Fury Is Often The Key To Miraculous Change.

⪦ 5 ⪧

WHAT GRIEVES YOU IS A CLUE TO SOMETHING YOU ARE ASSIGNED TO HEAL.

Tears talk.

What you cry about is a clue to something you were created and ordained by God to heal. *Compassion is a signpost.*

What grieves you? Battered wives? Abused and molested children? Ignorance? Disease? Poverty? Pornography? Homosexuality? Abortion? Name it. Be honest with yourself.

Caring qualifies you as an *instrument of healing.*

What makes you cry is a clue to a problem God has anointed you to change, conquer, and heal. Look at Nehemiah. His heart was broken about the walls of Jerusalem being broken down. He could not sleep at night. He could not rest. He wept long hours.

He was stirred with everything within him to write letters, contact officials, and even change his personal life to rebuild the walls.

Examine Ezra. His heart was broken over the temple in that city of Jerusalem. He could not rest. He wept and sobbed. He read Scriptures to the people. He knew that *the presence of God was the only remedy for wounded people.* He recognized that places mattered and that God would honor and reward those who sanctified a worship center in the city. *Those feelings* were signposts to his Assignment.

There is an insanity in our society. Observe how the liquor industry has their signs on every billboard of a stadium. Every newspaper is filled with liquor advertisements. Yet alcohol has murdered and destroyed more people on our streets and highways than those lost in the entire Vietnam war.

Someone has said that we have lost more of our children to death by alcoholism than every death combined in all the major wars. Yet everyone screams about the horrors of war while sipping their alcohol at a cocktail table.

Someday, God is going to raise up another Billy Sunday or someone who is tired of crying over children's brains splattered on a highway. Someone is going to be so grieved over senseless deaths that their Assignment becomes clear. Then, that Assignment will *become an obsession*, and he will rise up to launch a war...a holy war that will salvage the lives of thousands and *heal the broken* in this generation.

Have you wept long hours over financial bankruptcy and debt? Think of the many families in America who lack finances because of a father's drinking habit. Think of the children who cannot be put through school because money is wasted on alcohol. Do you weep when you see homeless children? Tears are clues to where God will use you the most.

Oh, there are many things that should set us on fire. What *grieves* you? What *saddens* you? What *moves you* to tears? Pay attention to it. *Tears are clues* to the nature of your Assignment.

Where You Hurt The Most Is A Clue To What You May Heal The Best.

⚭ 6 ⚭

WHAT YOU LOVE IS A CLUE TO THE GIFTS, SKILLS, AND WISDOM YOU CONTAIN.

Love births Wisdom.

Let me explain. When you have a love for children, a special Wisdom begins to grow and develop in you toward children. You begin to understand their fears, tears, and desires. When you have a love toward animals, you develop an intuition, a special Wisdom for their behavior and conduct. You can sense what they are feeling. When you need Wisdom in your marriage, love for your mate must be birthed first. *Wisdom is the product of love.*

Love births persistence. When you love something, you give birth to extraordinary tenacity, determination, and persistence. Recently, I read a powerful story about a runner. In his youth, he had a terrible disease. Doctors insisted he would never be able to even walk again. But something powerful was within him. *He loved running.*

His love for running birthed determination. He ended up winning a gold medal in the Olympics.

Love is stronger than sickness. It is stronger than disease. It is stronger than poverty.

So find what you truly and continuously love,

and *build your daily agenda around it.*

You contain certain qualities, specific gifts and worthy traits. They make you *unique.* You are distinct from the herd. What is it? What do you *love to talk about* the *most?*

I discussed this with my staff recently. "If every human on earth was paid $10 an hour for work, regardless of the type of job, what would you do? For example, if you chose to be a janitor of a building, you would receive $10 an hour for it. If you decided that you wanted to be a heart surgeon, you would still receive $10 an hour. What would you love to do if money was no longer a factor?" *That Is Your Life Assignment.*

Moses loved people. When he saw an Egyptian beating a fellow Israelite, he moved quickly. In his passion for justice he killed the Egyptian. That was unfortunate. It postponed his Assignment. But his love for his people was a clue to his mantle as a deliverer. He was attentive to the *cries. He cared.* His compassion ran deep. Because he had a love for people, he was able to lead people. They followed him. Yes, they complained, whined, and griped, but they had found their leader.

Abraham loved peace. He despised conflict. So when God decided to destroy Sodom and Gomorrah, Abraham became an intercessor and mediator for Lot, his nephew, who lived in Sodom. His love for peace and justice was rewarded by God. Though Sodom and Gomorrah were destroyed, Lot and his daughters were brought out safely. It happened because Abraham contained something very precious: a love for peace. *His love for peace birthed the Wisdom necessary to achieve it.*

Recently, a close friend of mine came to our ministry and gave a special teaching. He gave us a personality profile and helped us discover the greatest gifts within us. He showed us how to examine the lives of Bible characters and showed us how we relate to them. This is one of the most important things you can do. You must find what you really care about and develop your life around it.

It is wise to alter and change the flaws within us, but it is even wiser to acknowledge and embrace the center of your calling.

Permit the *true you* to become strong. I have often heard people insistently tell a shy person, "You must talk more!" Then the same person will turn to someone talking a lot and say, "Be quiet! Just sit and listen!" We instruct youth, "Get more serious about life." Then we instruct the elderly, "You need to be less serious and lighten up!"

Do not move away from the essence of what God made you. Understand the importance of your *uniqueness*.

Discern your gifts. *Name* your calling. Build your daily agenda around it. Whatever you are gifted to do is what you should be doing.

What you truly love the most is a clue to a marvelous gift and quality inside you.

≈ 7 ≈

YOUR ASSIGNMENT IS GEOGRAPHICAL.

Places matter.

God made places before He made people. Therefore where you are is as important as what you are.

Some time ago a minister friend shared an interesting story at lunch. "Mike," he said, "when I was 100 miles away from Dallas, I had fair success but nothing extraordinary. The moment I moved to Dallas, our church here absolutely exploded. I knew immediately that I was at the right place at the right time."

Where you are determines what grows within you. Your weaknesses or your strengths require a climate.

God spoke to Moses, "Ye have compassed this mountain long enough: turn you northward" (Deuteronomy 2:3).

Jesus knew that *geography mattered*. "And he must needs go through Samaria" (John 4:4). He could have added, "Because there is a woman there who needs Me, who will reach the entire city!"

Read John 4:1-42 carefully. Jesus knew that one person was in need of Him that very day.

Jonah was instructed to go to Nineveh. He rebelled. The whole world has since read his diary of attending "Whale University!"

Abraham was instructed to *leave* his father's house in Ur of the Chaldees and to set out for a *new land*.

Ruth left Moab and followed her mother-in-law Naomi *back to Bethlehem*, where she met her Boaz!

Esther was raised by Mordecai. But when God got ready to bless her, He moved *her into the palace*.

Five hundred were instructed by Jesus to go *to the upper room*. Only 120 obeyed. Only 120 got the promised blessing.

You cannot work on the wrong job, for the wrong boss, doing the wrong things for 40 hours a week and wonder why two hours per week in church does not change your life! *Geography plays a major part in every success story.*

God will not bless you just anywhere you go. God will bless you, however, if you are willing to go *anywhere* in order to *obey and please Him!* Yes, it is true: Where you are determines what grows within you—weeds or flowers, strengths or weaknesses.

Have you noticed that when you are in the presence of certain friends you laugh at different jokes? Have you noticed that the topic of your conversation often changes, depending on the person you are around?

Two Keys Have Unlocked Miracles For My Own Life:

1.   *Where You Are Determines Who Sees You.*
2.   *Those Who See You Determine The Favor That Comes Toward You.*

Nobody receives favor unless he is seen. Joseph did not get promoted until Pharaoh *saw* him. Ruth did not receive favor until Boaz *saw* her. The blind man received no instructions for healing until Jesus *saw* him. The daughter of Pharaoh did not show favor to baby Moses in the basket until she *saw* him.

Geography matters. It controls the *flow of favor* in your life. And never forget that *one day of favor is worth a thousand days of labor.*

Go where you are celebrated instead of where you are tolerated. Seek to be where God wants you, daily, hourly, weekly. Become more conscious of where you *are*, where you *work*, and for *whom* you work. It is so sad that some people simply take a newspaper and start calling places looking for a job instead of sitting in the presence of God and asking Him, "To *whom have I been sent today?"* Somebody is supposed to succeed *because of you.* Who is it? To *whom* have you been *sent?*

You see, *when you are with the right people, the best comes out of you* and the worse part of you will die.

Your success is always linked to a *place: the place of your Assignment.*

∼ 8 ∼

YOUR ASSIGNMENT WILL TAKE YOU WHERE YOU ARE CELEBRATED INSTEAD OF TOLERATED.

───────═⊃●⊂───────

Somebody, somewhere, sometime will celebrate you.

Jesus told His disciples, "And into whatsoever city or town ye shall enter, inquire who in it is worthy; and there abide till ye go thence. And when ye come into an house, salute it. And if the house be worthy, let your peace come upon it: but if it be not worthy, let your peace return to you. And whosoever shall not receive you, nor hear your words, when ye depart out of that house or city, shake off the dust of your feet" (Matthew 10:11-14).

Intimacy should be *earned*.

Jesus had different *Circles of Love* around Him. John, the beloved, laid his head on His shoulder. Peter, James, and John were the inner three. Then, the 12 disciples traveled with Him. Then there were the others and the multitudes.

The depth of desire determined the access He gave to others.

If you are in full-time ministry, take note: There was a time in my early ministry when I felt rejection quite keenly. When certain people did not accept me, I really felt like something must be wrong with me. Numerous times I have sat alone in my small motel room mentally replaying the service. Did I say something that disagreed with their theology? Did I say it the wrong way? Did I preach too long? Did I fail to give enough illustrations? Did they not like my singing?

There is no end to the doubts the enemy will put into your head about your life and your Assignment. Certainly it is good to evaluate your efforts, analyze your productivity, and strive to enter the highest level of excellence.

But when you study the life of Jesus, you do not see Him hungering for the approval of Pharisees. He would not move His little finger to attract hypocrites. Instead, He spent time with the ungodly tax collector who saw His value and celebrated His difference.

This may sound strong, but if you do not see yourself as a reward to others, you may become a whining wimp, crawling at the feet of snobbish and hypocritical people. Do not fall for that. Jesus said to test any house you enter. *Qualify people for your entry.* Ask yourself, "Are these people worthy of the gifts of God within me? Are they capable of celebrating the Treasure Who has just walked through the door?"

"Give not that which is holy unto the dogs, neither cast ye your pearls before swine, lest they trample them under their feet, and turn again and rend you" (Matthew 7:6).

Qualify the soil around you before planting the Seed of your life.

∼ 9 ∼

YOUR ASSIGNMENT WILL REQUIRE TIME.

━━━━━━━━━━━━

Time is the currency of earth.

The *peso* is the currency of Mexico. The *dollar* is the currency of the United States. The *franc* is the currency of France. The currency of earth is *Time*.

God did not give you friends. He gave you *Time,* and you *invested Time* into people and *created friendships.* He did not give you money. He gave you *Time.* You exchanged it for paper money from your boss and employer.

God uses Time to achieve His own goals on earth. He uses time to *develop* the Seeds of greatness He plants in the soil of people.

Your Assignment will require Time—more than you realize. It will require *preparation* time; seasons of *negotiation;* seasons of *insignificance;* seasons of *meditation;* seasons of *agitation.* And yes, even seasons of *warfare.*

Moses was trained by God for 80 years before becoming a great deliverer. Jesus invested 30 years of time before beginning His earthly ministry of three and one-half years.

"To every thing there is a season, and a time to every purpose under the heaven:

A time to be born, and a time to die; a time
    to plant, and a time to pluck up that
which is planted;
A time to kill, and a time to heal; a time to
    break down, and a time to build up;
A time to weep, and a time to laugh; a time
    to mourn, and a time to dance;
A time to cast away stones, and a time to
gather stones together; a time to embrace,
    and a time to refrain from embracing;
A time to get, and a time to lose; a time to
    keep, and a time to cast away;
A time to rend, and a time to sew; a time to
    keep silence, and a time to speak;
A time to love, and a time to hate; a time of
    war, and a time of peace"
                (Ecclesiastes 3:1-8).

"He hath made every thing beautiful in his time:
also he hath set the world in their heart, so that no
man can find out the work that God maketh from the
beginning to the end" (verse 11).

Greatness will cost you the currency of Time.

It takes *Time* to develop a relationship with your
mentor.

It takes *Time* to *establish a proven reputation* of
integrity.

It takes *Time* to carefully build a *financial
foundation* for a great future.

It takes *Time* to *extract information* from a crisis
or critical moment in your life.

It takes *Time* to be *restored* when you have made
a major mistake.

"And let us not be weary in well doing: for in due season we shall reap, if we faint not" (Galatians 6:9).

Someone has well said that it is impossible to *save* Time: You must simply learn to *invest* it wisely. "Redeeming the time, because the days are evil" (Ephesians 5:16).

Focus on creating a perfect day. You see, in a sense, you will never really see your future. When you arrive at your future, you will call it, "Today." Yesterday is *over*. Tomorrow is *not yet here*.

Yesterday is in the *tomb*.

Tomorrow is in the *womb*.

Today Is Really Your Life.

Use These Nine Keys To Make Your Time Count:

1. *Focus On Carefully Planning The Next 24 Hours.*

2. *Concentrate On Making Each Hour A Productive Hour.*

3. *Schedule An Hour Of Movement Toward Wisdom (Reading The Word Of God).*

4. *Schedule Another Hour Of Movement Toward The Holy Spirit And Receiving Counsel (Prayer Time In The Secret Place).*

5. *Schedule One Hour Of Movement Toward Health.* Exercise Daily.

6. *Schedule One Hour To Monitor, Mentor, And Motivate Your Love Circle.* These are those you love who are linked to your Assignment.

7. *Schedule An Hour For Restoration.* (It may be a nap or simply relaxing and watching the news

for a half hour. This is restoration time.)

8.   *Guard Access To Yourself.* Qualify those who enter your arena of life. They must desire *what you possess* or must *possess something you desire*.

9.   *Unclutter Your Life By Uncluttering Your Day.* Eliminate the things that God did not specifically tell you to do.

When you learn to create a perfect day, you can make it happen every day of your life.

Patience is often as powerful as faith. It is the force that makes faith productive. The patience of God has produced millions of saved lives. He was willing to patiently build a road into our lives until we found Him believable and accepted His authority in our life.

Take the time to discover your Assignment.

Then invest the time necessary to do it *right*.

∾ 10 ∾

IF YOU REBEL AGAINST YOUR ASSIGNMENT, GOD MAY PERMIT PAINFUL EXPERIENCES TO CORRECT YOU.

God will not be ignored.

God can create painful experiences, unforgettable experiences.

Jonah is a perfect example. He rebelled against God's instructions to "Arise, go to Nineveh, that great city, and cry against it; for their wickedness is come up before me" (Jonah 1:2). Instead he, "rose up to flee unto Tarshish from the presence of the Lord, and went down to Joppa; and he found a ship going to Tarshish: so he paid the fare thereof, and went down into it, to go with them unto Tarshish from the presence of the Lord. But the Lord sent out a great wind into the sea, and there was a mighty tempest in the sea, so that the ship was like to be broken" (verses 3,4).

Jonah had to endure three miserable days and nights in the belly of the fish before he came to his senses and *accepted* his Assignment.

Never misjudge God. Never think that He will

ignore tiny acts of defiance. Discipline comes. Reaction comes.

Look at the life of Joshua. When Achan rebelled and kept some of the spoils of war, they lost the first battle of Ai. In a single day, their reputation was stained, and Joshua's men lost total confidence. Achan had ignored the command of God. Consequently, the entire nation suffered defeat until obedience became their priority again.

Few have grasped this truth: *One person's disobedience can create corporate judgment.* It is possible that when one person is out of the will of God, everyone around that person *must pay the price for it.*

Years ago, a well-known leader made the statement that when finances became difficult for his ministry, he would go to prayer. One day God spoke to him to quit praying. "Someone is on your staff that has no business here. That is the reason I have closed the finances off." He fired that particular staff member, and the finances began to flow again. I said it earlier, but it should be said on every page of this book: *"When you get the wrong people out of your life, the wrong things stop happening."*

Remember, the waves of yesterday's disobedience will splash on the shores of today for a season. If you are walking in contradiction to God's laws, expect painful experiences on the road ahead.

Pain is corrective.

It happens often in the Potter's House, where our Father is remolding *common clay vessels for uncommon exploits.* "It is good for me that I have been afflicted; that I might learn Thy statutes" (Psalm 119:71).

There Are Five Rewards Of Pain:

1.   Pain Forces You To *Look*...To The Word Of God For Answers.

2.   Pain Forces You To *Lean*...On The Arm Of God, Instead Of Men.

3.   Pain Forces You To *Learn*...Where You Went Astray.

4.   Pain Forces You To *Long*...For His Presence And Healing.

5.   Pain Forces You To *Listen*...For Changes In God's Instructions.

So, do not misunderstand the hurting seasons. They birth the healing process.

≈ 11 ≈

GOD CAN FORGIVE ANY SIN OR MISTAKE YOU HAVE MADE IN PURSUIT OF YOUR ASSIGNMENT.

Failure occurs. God is not surprised by it.

God knows that men fall. "The steps of a good man are ordered by the Lord: and He delighteth in his way. Though he fall, he shall not be utterly cast down: for the Lord upholdeth him with His hand" (Psalm 37:23,24).

Good men sometimes fall more than once. "For a just man falleth seven times, and riseth up again" (Proverbs 24:16).

Those who walked with Jesus daily even failed. Jesus predicted it. Listen to what He told Peter, "Verily, verily, I say unto thee, The cock shall not crow, till thou hast denied Me thrice" (John 13:38). It happened. "Peter then denied again: and immediately the cock crew" (John 18:27).

Jesus did not condemn him, criticize him nor destroy him. He simply forgave him. Then He turned Peter into one of the most magnificent and powerful soul winners recorded in the New Testament. "Then

Peter said unto them, Repent, and be baptized every one of you in the name of Jesus Christ for the remission of sins...Then they that gladly received his word were baptized: and the same day there were added unto them about three thousand souls" (Acts 2:38, 41). He even went on to write two more books in the New Testament!

First, Jesus birthed *hope* in Peter by showing him a photograph of his *future victories* as well. "And I say also unto thee, That thou art Peter, and upon this rock I will build My church; and the gates of hell shall not prevail against it" (Matthew 16:18).

Then Jesus sowed into his life the very keys of the kingdom. "And I will give unto thee the keys of the kingdom of heaven: and whatsoever thou shalt bind on earth shall be bound in heaven: and whatsoever thou shalt loose on earth shall be loosed in heaven" (Matthew 16:19).

Then, Jesus *alerted him to his enemy*, to increase Peter's caution and guardedness. "And the Lord said, Simon, Simon, behold, Satan hath desired to have you, that he may sift you as wheat" (Luke 22:31).

Then Jesus promised to become his *personal intercessor*, to pray for him. "But I have prayed for thee, that thy faith fail not" (Luke 22:32).

Last, Jesus *gave him an Assignment* that showed His personal confidence that Peter would complete it. "And when thou art converted, strengthen thy brethren" (Luke 22:32).

One of the saddest and most heartbreaking chapters in the entire Bible is 2 Samuel 11. One of the greatest champions of the faith, David, fell into immorality. First, he committed the sin of adultery with Bathsheba. Then, he went one step further: He decided to have her husband murdered in battle.

But, the man of God showed up at his house.

Penalties always occur. If you never saw God penalize rebellion, it would be impossible to have faith that He would reward obedience. Judgment did come. A child died. A son raped a daughter. Another son had his brother killed.

But David had an ability that surpassed his capability on the harp. It surpassed his ability as a warrior on the battle field. He possessed an ability that superseded his management skills of supervising the entire kingdom.

David had the *ability to repent.*

"And David said unto Nathan, I have sinned against the Lord. And Nathan said unto David, the Lord also hath put away thy sin; thou shalt not die" (2 Samuel 12:13).

Have you failed? Is your heart broken over your mistake? A Royal Invitation has been sent to your house today. "Come now, and let us reason together, saith the Lord: though your sins be as scarlet, they shall be as white as snow; though they be red like crimson, they shall be as wool" (Isaiah 1:18).

Samson is a familiar story of failure. Many do not recall his recovery. His story is a collection of miracles. An angel of the Lord appeared to his mother and predicted his birth. She was instructed to discipline his life carefully because God had selected him to be a deliverer for Israel. (See Judges 13:2-5.)

God blessed him. The Spirit of the Lord came upon him, and he had supernatural experiences when his strength was miraculous. (See Judges 14:6, 19.)

Enemies targeted his life. They ambushed him. They carefully planned his downfall. They found his weakness—a woman. She was sensuous. She was manipulative. She was a pawn in the hand of his enemies. She was tenacious and persistent every single day.

She wanted him to empty his heart and tell the deepest secret of his life. "And it came to pass, when she pressed him daily with her words, and urged him, so that his soul was vexed unto death; That he told her all his heart, and said unto her, There hath not come a razor upon mine head; for I have been a Nazarite unto God from my mother's womb: if I be shaven, then my strength will go from me, and I shall become weak, and be like any other man" (Judges 16:16,17).

He failed in a tragic and horrifying way. "But the Philistines took him, and put out his eyes, and brought him down to Gaza, and bound him with fetters of brass; and he did grind in the prison house" (Judges 16:21).

However, seasons began to change. "Howbeit the hair of his head began to grow again after he was shaven" (Judges 16:22).

When they brought him in to make sport of him in the big auditorium, *Samson remembered yesterday.*

He remembered the *presence of God*.

He recalled his anointing and electrifying victories.

Somehow, he *knew* the heart of God.

He reached again. Oh, it is a fantastic day in your life when you make the decision to *reach back* for restoration. God has been *waiting for you*. Like the

MIKE MURDOCK ■ 43

father of the prodigal son, He will run to meet you at the gate! Oh yes, He will!

"And Samson called unto the Lord, and said, O Lord God, remember me, I pray Thee, and strengthen me, I pray Thee, only this once, O God, that I may be at once avenged of the Philistines for my two eyes. And Samson said, Let me die with the Philistines. And he bowed himself with all his might; and the house fell upon the lords, and upon all the people that were therein. So the dead which he slew at his death were more than they which he slew in his life" (Judges 16:28,30).

And that is not the end of the story. He is mentioned hundreds and hundreds of years later when God unfolded the heroes of faith in Hebrews 11. He is mentioned in the same chapter with Abraham, Isaac, Jacob, Joseph, Moses and Samuel the prophet. "And what shall I more say? for the time would fail Me to tell of Gedeon, and of Barak, and of Samson, and of Jephthae; of David also, and Samuel, and of the prophets: Who through faith subdued kingdoms, wrought righteousness, obtained promises, stopped the mouths of lions, Quenched the violence of fire, escaped the edge of the sword, out of weakness were made strong, waxed valiant in fight, turned to flight the armies of the aliens" (Hebrews 11:32-34).

God did it for Samson. And, *He can do it for you*.

In Hebrews, the name of Bathsheba is never mentioned. The name of Delilah is never discussed. You see, yesterday is over. It is ended. "Remember ye not the former things, neither consider the things of old. Behold, I will do a new thing; now it shall spring forth; shall ye not know it? I will even make a way in

the wilderness, and rivers in the desert"   (Isaiah
43:18,19).

Your responsibility is to *reach*.

God's responsibility is to *respond*.

"For as the heaven is high above the earth, so
great is His mercy toward them that fear Him. As far
as the east is from the west, so far hath He removed
our transgressions from us. Like as a father pitieth
his children, so the Lord pitieth them that fear Him.
For He knoweth our frame; He remembereth that we
are dust. But the mercy of the Lord is from everlasting
to everlasting upon them that fear Him, and His
righteousness unto children's children" (Psalm 103:11-
14,17).

You must focus *again* on your Assignment. Your
best days are *just ahead*.

∾ 12 ∾

Your Assignment Will Require Seasons Of Preparation.

You are not born qualified—you must become qualified.

Look at the life of Moses. He spent his first 40 years learning the Wisdom of the Egyptians. "And Moses was learned in all the Wisdom of the Egyptians, and was mighty in words and in deeds. And when he was full forty years old, it came into his heart to visit his brethren the children of Israel" (Acts 7:22,23).

He spent another 40 years learning the lessons of leadership and priesthood. "Now Moses kept the flock of Jethro his father in law, the priest of Midian: and he led the flock to the backside of the desert, and came to the mountain of God, even to Horeb"   (Exodus 3:1).

"And when forty years were expired, there appeared to him in the wilderness of mount Sina an angel of the Lord in a flame of fire in a bush. When Moses saw it, he wondered at the sight: and as he drew near to behold it, the voice of the Lord came unto him" (Acts 7:30,31).

Moses was a protégé for 80 years. During his first 40 years, he was a general in the Egyptian army.

During his second 40 years, he was a shepherd of hundreds of sheep.

Preparation. *Preparation.* PREPARATION.

Jesus spent 30 years preparing for His ministry. "And Jesus himself began to be about thirty years of age" (Luke 3:23). These days seem so different for young ministers. The average young minister wants to prepare for three-and-a-half years for 30 years of public ministry. Jesus did the opposite. *He prepared for 30 years for a public ministry of three and a half years.*

The Apostle Paul was a Pharisee and the son of a Pharisee. (See Acts 23:6.) He had invested years of preparation for the intelligentsia of his generation. "If any other man thinketh that he hath whereof he might trust in the flesh, I more: Circumcised the eighth day, of the stock of Israel, of the tribe of Benjamin, an Hebrew of the Hebrews; as touching the law, a Pharisee; Concerning zeal, persecuting the church; touching the righteousness which is in the law, blameless" (Philippians 3:4-6).

Yet that was not enough preparation. "But what things were gain to me, those I counted loss for Christ" (verse 7).

God had another three-year school for him. "Neither went I up to Jerusalem to them which were apostles before me; but I went into Arabia, and returned again unto Damascus. Then after three years I went up to Jerusalem to see Peter, and abode with him fifteen days" (Galatians 1:17,18).

Paul Mentored Others Concerning 14 Seasons Of Life In The Ministry:

1.   Seasons Of *Affliction*—"Be thou partaker of the afflictions of the gospel according to the power of God" (2 Timothy 1:8). "It is good for me that I have been afflicted; that I might learn Thy statutes" (Psalm 119:71).

2.   Seasons Of *Solitude*—"Greatly desiring to see Thee, being mindful of thy tears, that I may be filled with joy" (2 Timothy 1:4).

3.   Seasons Of *Warfare*—"Thou therefore endure hardness, as a good soldier of Jesus Christ. No man that warreth entangleth himself with the affairs of this life; that he may please Him who hath chosen him to be a soldier" (2 Timothy 2:3,4).

4.   Seasons Of *Suffering*—"If we suffer, we shall also reign with Him: if we deny Him, He also will deny us" (2 Timothy 2:12).

5.   Seasons Of *Ignorance*—"Study to show thyself approved unto God, a workman that needeth not to be ashamed, rightly dividing the word of truth" (2 Timothy 2:15).

6.   Seasons Of *Carnal Desires*—"Flee also youthful lusts: but follow righteousness, faith, charity, peace, with them that call on the Lord out of a pure heart" (2 Timothy 2:22).

7.   Seasons Of *Contention*—"But foolish and unlearned questions avoid, knowing that they do gender strifes. And the servant of the Lord must not strive; but be gentle unto all men, apt to teach, patient" (2 Timothy 2:23,24).

8.   Seasons Of *Persecution*—"Persecutions,

afflictions, which came unto me...what persecutions I endured: but out of them all the Lord delivered me. Yea, and all that will live godly in Christ Jesus shall suffer persecution" (2 Timothy 3:11,12).

9. Seasons Of *Proving Yourself*—"But watch thou in all things, endure afflictions, do the work of an evangelist, make full proof of thy ministry" (2 Timothy 4:5).

10. Seasons Of *Disloyalty*—"For Demas hath forsaken me, having loved this present world, and is departed unto Thessalonica" (2 Timothy 4:10).

11. Seasons Of *Injustice*—"Alexander the coppersmith did me much evil: the Lord reward him according to his works" (2 Timothy 4:14).

12. Seasons Of *Isolation*—"At my first answer no man stood with me, but all man forsook me: I pray God that it may not be laid to their charge" (2 Timothy 4:16).

13. Seasons Of *Supernatural Intervention*— "Notwithstanding the Lord stood with me, and strengthened me; that by me the preaching might be fully known, and that all the Gentiles might hear" (2 Timothy 4:17).

14. Seasons Of *Deliverance*—"I was delivered out of the mouth of the lion. And the Lord shall deliver me from every evil work, and will preserve me unto His heavenly kingdom: to whom be glory for ever and ever" (2 Timothy 4:17,18).

In every season, He walked in *Victory*. (See Romans 8:35-39.)

As I review the 50 years of my life, I see many seasons. In each season, I felt ignorant and unaware of the *purpose* of that specific season. I would wonder,

"How could God get any glory out of this situation?" Looking back, I see His divine intervention. He taught me so much.

Did you ever see the movie, "The Karate Kid"? It contains some powerful lessons. In the story, the young boy desperately wanted to learn the art of fighting. His old mentor waited, and instead handed him a paint brush and instructed him to paint the fence. The young man was disheartened, but he followed the instructions of his mentor.

Discouraged, disillusioned, and very disappointed, he could not see any relationship between painting the fence and fighting in the ring. When he finished, he was instructed to wash, wax, and polish the car. As he moved his hands in a circular motion over the car, he was very demoralized. His thoughts were, "How will this help me in my future? How will this help me achieve my desire to be a great fighter?"

But the old mentor was secretly preparing each motion of his hands to *develop the hands of a fighter.* The young man did not discern it until much later.

Your heavenly Father knows what He is doing with your life. "But He knoweth the way that I take: when He hath tried me, I shall come forth as gold" (Job 23:10).

Sometimes you will not discern His presence. "Behold, I go forward, but He is not there; and backward, but I cannot perceive Him: On the left hand, where He doth work, but I cannot behold Him: He hideth Himself on the right hand, that I cannot see Him" (Job 23:8,9).

Yes, you will even experience seasons of chastening.

"For whom the Lord loveth He chasteneth, and scourgeth every son whom He receiveth. Now no chastening for the present seemeth to be joyous, but grievous: nevertheless afterward it yieldeth the peaceable fruit of righteousness unto them which are exercised thereby" (Hebrews 12:6,11).

So fully embrace and have expectation of the *present season* God has scheduled in your life. *Extract every possible benefit.* "Wherefore lift up the hands which hang down, and the feeble knees" (Hebrews 12:12).

You will survive the fires of the furnace. "Though I walk in the midst of trouble, Thou wilt revive me: Thou shalt stretch forth Thine hand against the wrath of mine enemies, and Thy right hand shall save me" (Psalm 138:7).

You are being perfected for your Assignment. "The Lord will perfect that which concerneth me" (Psalm 138:8).

Your success is inevitable.

~ 13 ~

Your Assignment May Contain Seasons Of Insignificance.

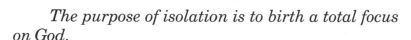

The purpose of isolation is to birth a total focus on God.

You see, *the only reason men fail is broken focus.* When satan wants to distract you, he brings someone into your life to break your attention off God. So, the Father in His incredible Wisdom knows how to remove those distractions and cause us to behold Him again.

Seven Facts About Seasons Of Insignificance:

1.	*You May Experience Spiritual Isolation From Someone Who Labors With You In The Work Of God.* "For Demas hath forsaken me, having loved this present world, and is departed unto Thessalonica" (2 Timothy 4:10).

2.	*You May Experience Social Isolation And Loss Of Respect In Your Community.* "By faith Moses, when he was come to years, refused to be called the son of Pharaoh's daughter; Choosing rather to suffer affliction with the people of God, than to enjoy the pleasures of sin for a season; Esteeming the reproach of Christ greater riches than the treasures in Egypt: for he had respect unto the recompense of the reward" (Hebrews 11:24-26).

3. *You May Experience Bankruptcy And Financial Isolation From Everything That Was Secure In Your Life.* It happened to Job. "And there came a messenger unto Job, and said, The oxen were plowing, and the asses feeding beside them: And the Sabeans fell upon them, and took them away; yea, they have slain the servants with the edge of the sword" (Job 1:14,15). "While he was yet speaking, there came also another, and said, The Chaldeans made out three bands, and fell upon the camels, and have carried them away" (Job 1:17).

4. *The Seasons Will Change.* "And the Lord turned the captivity of Job, when he prayed for his friends: also the Lord gave Job twice as much as he had before" (Job 42:10).

5. *Endurance Is Rewarded. Always.* That is why Paul encouraged, "Cast not away therefore your confidence, which hath great recompense of reward. For ye have need of patience, that, after ye have done the will of God, ye might receive the promise" (Hebrews 10:35,36).

6. *God Reveals The Purpose Of Seasons.* "And thou shalt remember all the way which the Lord thy God led thee these forty years in the wilderness, to humble thee, and to prove thee, to know what was in thine heart, whether thou wouldest keep His commandments, or no...that He might make thee know that man doth not live by bread only, but by every word that proceedeth out of the mouth of the

Lord doth man live" (Deuteronomy 8:2,3).
    7.   *Your Next Season Is A Season Of Blessing.*
He guaranteed it. "For the Lord thy God bringeth thee into a good land, a land of brooks of water, of fountains and depths that spring out of valleys and hills; A land of wheat, and barley, and vines, and fig trees, and pomegranates; a land of oil olive, and honey; A land wherein thou shalt eat bread without scarceness, thou shalt not lack any thing in it" (Deuteronomy 8:7-9).
    He did it for Israel.
    He will do it for *you.*

❧ 14 ❧

YOUR ASSIGNMENT MAY REQUIRE SEASONS OF WAITING.

Waiting is proof of trust.

There Are 13 Rewards In Waiting On God:

1. *Waiting Reveals Patience.* Patience is a Seed. It always produces a desired Harvest. Patience is always *rewarded.* "Through faith also Sara herself received strength to conceive Seed, and was delivered of a child when she was past age, because she judged Him faithful who had promised" (Hebrews 11:11).

2. *Waiting Time Is Not Wasted Time.* "But let patience have her perfect work, that ye may be perfect and entire, wanting nothing" (James 1:4).

3. *Waiting Guarantees Favorable Results.* "The Lord is good unto them that wait for Him, to the soul that seeketh Him. It is good that a man should both hope and quietly wait for the salvation of the Lord" (Lamentations 3:25,26).

4. *Waiting Is Learning Time.* As long as you are learning, you are not losing. Your Assignment will require *warfare.* Battles are normal on the field of

your Assignment. The integrity of the general demands that he qualify his soldiers for the battle. God will train and teach you in the waiting time. "Blessed be the Lord my strength, which teacheth my hands to war, and my fingers to fight" (Psalm 144:1).

Your flesh will react to waiting. It hates waiting. It wants action. It pursues activity. *Waiting forces it to die.*

5. *Waiting Will Reveal The True Motives And Intentions Of Those Around You.* Motives are not always easily discerned. That is why Joseph was willing to wait before revealing his identity to his brothers when they approached him for food.

They did not know he was their brother. He knew them. Undoubtedly, the desire to reveal himself was intense. But he knew the limitations of intuition. He remembered the excitement of sharing his dream with his brothers, only to be sold into slavery because of it.

Wise men never trust their intuition. They rely on *tests*.

The young *trust*.

The wise *test*.

6. *Waiting Reveals That You Trust God But Are Willing To Test Men.* It is biblical. "Some trust in chariots, and some in horses: but we will remember the name of the Lord our God" (Psalm 20:7). You see, wrong people can keep their mistakes covered for long periods of time. Waiting forces the truth to emerge.

7. *Waiting Enables You To Gather Accurate And Untainted Information.* And the quality of your information determines the quality of your decisions. The quality of your decisions determines the quality of your life.

8. *Waiting Brings You Truth.*

9.   *More Waiting Brings You More Truth.*

10.   *Enough Waiting Brings You Enough Truth.*

11.   *Waiting Provides God Time To Address Your Problem Miraculously.* God is a miracle God. When you get ahead of Him, you rob Him of an opportunity to prove His power in your life. You will never see the hand of God if you keep trusting the hand of man in your life. Unwillingness to wait for supernatural provision will produce tragedy every time.

If you could attend the workshop of Abraham, you would hear him weep and tell you a thousand times, "Do not birth an Ishmael in your life. Wait for the timing of God. He will always fulfill His promise."

Your Father knows you very well. He is not faint. He is not weary. There is no limit to His understanding.

12.   *Waiting Increases Strength.* "He giveth power to the faint; and to them that have no might He increaseth strength. Even the youths shall faint and be weary, and the young men shall utterly fall: But they that wait upon the Lord shall renew their strength; they shall mount up with wings as eagles; they shall run, and not be weary; and they shall walk, and not faint" (Isaiah 40:29-31).

13.   *Waiting Is A Weapon* Satan Dreads For You To Ever Discover. "Lest Satan should get an advantage of us: for we are not ignorant of his devices" (2 Corinthians 2:11).

≈ 15 ≈

YOUR ASSIGNMENT MAY REQUIRE SEASONS OF ISOLATION.

It is natural to desire the presence of others.

However, there will be moments in the pursuit of your Assignment when you feel totally alienated *from those you love.* It will appear they do not understand. It will seem that you alone are motivated to complete the instructions for your own life.

Jesus may have felt this way immediately following His baptism. "Then was Jesus led up of the Spirit into the wilderness to be tempted of the devil. And when He had fasted forty days and forty nights, He was afterward an hungered" (Matthew 4:1,2).

The tempter times his temptations.

Satan does not attend baptisms. At Jesus' baptism, the *crowd* was there. The *motivation* was there. The currents of joy were like a flurry of clouds around Him. No, satan waited until Jesus was *alone and isolated* from the encouragement of *others*.

Almost every major satanic attack will occur when you are alone.

So why does God permit you to be alone? Those are the moments when He reveals His presence, His purpose, His plan, and His power.

When you are listening only to others, you may not hear God speaking to you. Isolation is more than emotional emptiness. It provokes absolute dependence upon *the Holy Spirit.* It is during these times that you *develop an addiction to His presence,* which is the only true proof of *maturity.*

When David was isolated and separated from his family, tending sheep, God gave him victories *nobody else observed.* "And David said unto Saul, Thy servant kept his father's sheep, and there came a lion, and a bear, and took a lamb out of the flock: And I went out after him, and smote him, and delivered it out of his mouth: and when he arose against me, I caught him by his beard, and smote him, and slew him. Thy servant slew both the lion and the bear" (1 Samuel 17:34-36).

Ministers feel isolated when their message is misunderstood and not embraced.

Mothers feel isolated when a father will not back them up in their instruction to the children.

Fathers feel isolated when their labors are ignored and unappreciated.

Employees feel isolated when only their mistakes are acknowledged.

Children feel isolated when parents are too busy to stop and focus on their conversations.

Husbands feel isolated when their wives show more excitement over their children than they do over them.

Wives feel isolated when husbands would rather work overtime than be with their family.

I have known many times of isolation throughout my fifty years of living. Sometimes I have made the mistake of *searching out a substitute for His presence*. Perhaps I would sit down and watch television to distract and break my focus off the emptiness within me. Sometimes I have reached for the telephone to call a friend.

The most important thing you can do during moments of isolation is *reach for the One Who awaits you*. He wants to be *pursued*. He craves *relationship*. "Call unto Me, and I will answer thee, and shew thee great and mighty things, which thou knowest not" (Jeremiah 33:3).

You are on His mind. "For I know the thoughts that I think toward you, saith the Lord, thoughts of peace, and not of evil, to give you an expected end. Then shall ye call upon Me, and ye shall go and pray unto Me, and I will hearken unto you. And ye shall seek Me, and find Me, when ye shall search for Me with all your heart" (Jeremiah 29:11-13).

You will find Him during times of isolation. "And I will be found of you, saith the Lord: and I will turn away your captivity" (Jeremiah 29:14).

Seasons of isolation pass. But they are important in revealing the *limitations* of our loved ones. These seasons reveal the deep need we have for God, and they fuel and nurture a continuous focus on Him for our Assignment.

Private victories can birth *public* victories.

Private victories can lead to *public* honor.

Those times build *character*.

Those times birth *revelation* of the power of God.

Those times of vulnerability create an *obsession with His presence*.

～ 16 ～

PEOPLE WILL BE ASSIGNED BY HELL TO DISTRACT, DELAY, DISCOURAGE, AND DERAIL YOUR ASSIGNMENT.

You will not go unhindered.

Recently, I was sitting in the office of a pastor. Several of the ministers were discussing their most recent project.

"Dr. Murdock, it must be God. Everything is falling into place perfectly. There has been no struggle, no conflict whatsoever. That is how we know God is in it."

Some champions feel differently. "Women received their dead raised to life again: and others were tortured, not accepting deliverance; that they might obtain a better resurrection: And others had trial of cruel mockings and scourgings, yea, moreover of bonds and imprisonment: They were stoned, they were sawn asunder, were tempted, were slain with the sword: they wandered about in sheepskins and goatskins; being destitute, afflicted, tormented; (Of whom the world was not worthy:) they wandered in deserts, and in mountains, and in dens and caves of the earth" (Hebrews 11:35-38).

The apostle Paul experienced hindrances. "...in stripes above measure, in prisons more frequent, in deaths oft. Of the Jews five times received I forty stripes save one. Thrice was I beaten with rods, once was I stoned, thrice I suffered shipwreck, a night and a day I have been in the deep; In journeyings often, in perils of waters, in perils of robbers, in perils by mine own countrymen, in perils by the heathen, in perils in the city, in perils in the wilderness, in perils in the sea, in perils among false brethren; In weariness and painfulness, in watchings often, in hunger and thirst, in fastings often, in cold and nakedness" (2 Corinthians 11:23-27).

Jesus expected adversity: "The foxes have holes, and the birds of the air have nests; but the Son of man hath not where to lay His head" (Matthew 8:20).

"Then shall they deliver you up to be afflicted, and shall kill you: and ye shall be hated of all nations for My name's sake" (Matthew 24:9).

"Remember the word that I said unto you, the servant is not greater than his lord. If they have persecuted Me, they will also persecute you" (John 15:20).

Some enemies are known enemies of the Cross. They are global, international, and well known. Their influence is political and social. They are often articulate, brilliant and masters of satire, cynicism, and sarcasm. Their words are sneering, poisonous, and contentious to ministers, Christians, and to those who believe in the infallibility of Scripture.

They are dedicated to destroying the faith of people. They are masters at *disguise.* They *appear* to be in pursuit of truth, and want to "expose" the hypocrisy of religion. However, they do not restore the fallen, heal the wounded, or liberate those who are on drugs and alcohol. *They are weapons in the hands of satan.*

Their goal is the ruin of anything godly. They are fueled and energized by demonic influence and their own fleshly nature which "lusteth against the Spirit." (See Galatians 5:17.)

They are infuriated when children want to pray in a public classroom. They scheme, strategize, and plan the destruction of every Christian television and radio station in America. They bond with everything ungodly that is in opposition to the pure Word of God.

They influence congressmen. They intimidate presidents. They support the parading of homosexuality. They support the daily practice of murdering babies in America called abortion. They work day and night to distract ministers from focusing on the preaching of the Gospel.

These are global influences that must become the target of our faith and prayers.

It is unwise to ignore them.

It is *dangerous* to retaliate.

It is folly to change your focus.

Seven Important Facts To Remember When Facing Enemies Of The Cross:

1. *It Is Important To Become Aware, Alert, And Articulate Regarding Your Position Of Rights And Faith As Christians.* "But sanctify the Lord God in your hearts: and be ready always to give an answer to every man that asketh you a reason of the hope that is in you with meekness and fear" (1 Peter 3:15).

2. *It Is Important To Be Strong, Stand Unafraid, And Refuse To Be Intimidated.* "But and if ye suffer for righteousness' sake, happy are ye: and be not afraid of their terror, neither be troubled" (1 Peter 3:14).

3. *It Is Important To Fully Depend On The Capability Of The Holy Spirit To Answer Powerfully In The Halls Of Government.* "And when they bring you unto the synagogues, and unto magistrates, and powers, take ye no thought how or what thing ye shall answer, or what ye shall say: For the Holy Ghost shall teach you in the same hour what ye ought to say" (Luke 12:11,12).

4. *It Is Important To Enter Into Prayerful Agreement With Other Believers Across The World.* "Verily I say unto you, Whatsoever ye shall bind on earth shall be bound in heaven: and whatsoever ye shall loose on earth shall be loosed in heaven. Again I say unto you, That if two of you shall agree on earth as touching any thing that they shall ask, it shall be done for them of My Father which is in heaven. For where two or three are gathered together in My name, there am I in the midst of them" (Matthew 18:18-20).

5. *It Is Important To Target Kings, Presidents, Congressmen, And Leaders Of Nations With Our Faith In God.* "I exhort therefore, that, first of all, supplications, prayers, intercessions, and giving of thanks, be made for all men; For kings, and for all that are in authority; that we may lead a quiet and peaceable life in all godliness and honesty. For this is good and acceptable in the sight of God our Saviour;" (1 Timothy 2:1-3).

6. *It Is Important To Remember That God Wants Every One Of These Enemies To Become Believers, Born Again And Changed By His Power.* "Who will have all men to be saved, and to come unto the knowledge of the truth" (1 Timothy 2:4). "The Lord is not slack concerning His promise, as some men count slackness; but is longsuffering to us-ward, not willing that any should perish, but that all should come to repentance" (2 Peter 3:9).

7. *It Is Important To Expect Your Faith To Produce Changes.* Your faith works. My faith works. Together, you and I can see many miracles launched across the earth. It happened in the Book of Acts.

The *tormentor* of the early church was named Saul. He was present and consenting to the death of Stephen as he was being stoned. (See Acts 7:58,59; 8:1.)

Saul was a destroyer. "As for Saul, he made havock of the church, entering into every house, and haling men and women committed them to prison" (Acts 8:3).

This tormentor networked with other political leaders to destroy the body of Christ. "And Saul, yet breathing out threatenings and slaughter against the disciples of the Lord, went unto the high priest, And desired of him letters to Damascus to the synagogues, that if he found any of this way, whether they were men or women, he might bring them bound unto Jerusalem" (Acts 9:1,2).

Tormentors can be stopped, changed, and delivered, too. "And as he journeyed, he came near Damascus: and suddenly there shined round about him a light from heaven: And he fell to the earth, and heard a voice saying unto him, Saul, Saul, why persecutest thou Me? And he said, Who art Thou, Lord? And the Lord said, I am Jesus whom thou persecutest: it is hard for thee to kick against the pricks" (Acts 9:3-5).

Tormentors can be turned around instantly. "And he trembling and astonished said, Lord, what wilt Thou have me to do?" (Acts 9:6).

Tormentors have an Assignment also, and it can be unlocked and discovered. "And the Lord said unto him, Arise, and go into the city, and it shall be told thee what thou must do" (Acts 9:6).

It only takes one moment to reverse the philosophy of a tormentor. "And Saul arose from the earth; and when his eyes were opened, he saw no man: but they led him by the hand, and brought him into Damascus. And he was three days without sight, and neither did eat nor drink" (Acts 9:8,9). God made him blind. He entered a fast immediately for three days. He was shocked, stunned, and changed.

The tormentor of the church became the tormentor of hell.

This tormentor of the world became the mentor of the Church.

Those who appear rebellious, wild, and hateful are leaders misplaced from their Assignment. You and I can become their intercessors. God will intervene. He is looking for another Ananias who will go and pray for a Saul. (Read Acts 9:10-20.)

God is searching for intercessors. They will make the difference in this generation and the next. "And I sought for a man among them, that should make up the hedge, and stand in the gap before Me for the land, that I should not destroy it: but I found none" (Ezekiel 22:30).

Leaders have followers. When leaders are awakened to the truth, many followers will discover that same Jesus. I encourage you in this: When you are watching television and observing defiant, articulate, and rebellious leaders of the world, stretch forth your hand toward them and pray this prayer: "Heavenly Father, I ask You to put spiritual voices close to their ears. Convict them deeply of sin and rebellion within their heart. Turn their lives around. Use favor, disaster, or disease, any weapon necessary to awaken them toward You. In the name of Jesus, let them have the same kind of experience that Saul had on the road to Damascus. Save them, and cause them to be a great influence for You. In Jesus' name. Amen."

My father was a pastor while I was growing up. He changed pastorates quite often, so our family moved around a lot. This meant constant changing of schools. I was uncomfortable in every new town, but I learned something pretty quickly. When other boys would gather round, everyone followed a leader in the group. If he was a bully, I discovered early the benefits of whipping him that very day. I knew I could not take on the whole gang. I would lose. But there was always one ringleader. If I won his respect, the rest of the guys would follow without question. So when I entered a new school, I only had one major difficulty—with the bully. A little blood, a little pain, and then school was fine.

I have seen this happen in families. When the *intercessor for the family targets his or her faith on the patriarch of the family*, or whoever has the most influence in that household, the rest of the family eventually follows. Too often, we use our efforts in faith to focus on those who appear to be close to making a decision for Christ. It would be dramatic and powerful to see what would happen if the entire body of Christ focused our faith on the spokespersons of our generation, those who are determined to destroy the faith of our youth.

You may have to confront other voices closer to you and your home. Some of these voices will refuse your efforts to share Jesus with them. They will taunt and laugh. Paul understood this. And he released them to the judgment of God. "Alexander the coppersmith did me much evil: the Lord reward him according to his works" (2 Timothy 4:14).

Some who reject correction repeatedly must be left alone to the judgments and penalties of God. "A man that is an heretick after the first and second admonition reject; Knowing that he that is such is subverted, and sinneth, being condemned of himself" (Titus 3:10,11).

You cannot force people to come to Christ. Jesus taught the disciples to qualify people for association, fellowship, and intimacy. "And into whatsoever city or town ye shall enter, inquire who in it is worthy; and there abide till ye go thence. And when ye come into an house, salute it. And if the house be worthy, let your peace come upon it: but if it be not worthy, let your peace return to you. And whosoever shall not receive you, nor hear your words, when ye depart out of that house or city, shake off the dust of your feet" (Matthew 10:11-14).

Permit God to judge and penalize others. "Verily

I say unto you, It shall be more tolerable for the land of Sodom and Gomorrha in the day of judgment, than for that city" (Matthew 10:15).

Sometimes those of your own household become your greatest enemies to your own Assignment. "And a man's foes shall be they of his own household" (Matthew 10:36). Joseph experienced this when his own brothers sold him as a slave to a passing band of Ishmaelites. Job experienced this through his own wife. In the most devastating tragedy he had ever known, she refused to encourage him. "Then said his wife unto him, Dost thou still retain thine integrity? curse God, and die" (Job 2:9).

Job responded sincerely to his wife. He refused to be influenced away from God by her. He fought for his focus. "But he said unto her, Thou speakest as one of the foolish women speaketh" (Job 2:10).

Sometimes satan uses your closest friends to scrutinize your flaws unmercifully and to demoralize you. Job experienced this from his three friends who tried to destroy him emotionally. They tried to do to him emotionally what satan had done to him financially and physically. They blamed him for his own circumstances.

Here Are Six Important Keys To Help You When Someone Close To You Threatens To Break Your Focus From Your Assignment:

1.   *Remember That God's Assignment For Your Life Is Permanent* And Cannot Be Altered By Those Who Do Not Understand You.

2. *Spend More Time In The Secret Place* Hearing From The Holy Spirit Then You Do Sitting At The Tables Of Others, Hearing Their Insults And Opinions.

3. *Remember The Inner Dream* God Has Burned Into Your Spirit. Joseph did this, and he saw the big picture of God throughout his tragedies.

4.   *Reach For Intercessors* Who Are Godly, Mature, And Compassionate. "Again I say unto you, That if two of you shall agree on earth as touching any thing that they shall ask, it shall be done for them of My Father which is in heaven" (Matthew 18:19).

5. *Withdraw From Wrong People.* Remember Samson, who was blinded because he permitted the wrong person to get too close to him. *It only takes one person to destroy your Assignment.*

6. *Absorb The Continuous Flow Of Wisdom* At The Feet Of Your God-Given Mentor. "He that walketh with wise men shall be wise: but a companion of fools shall be destroyed" (Proverbs 13:20).

You can lose in one day what took you twenty years to build. Do not risk it.

Fight any battle necessary to maintain your focus.

❧ 17 ❧

YOUR ASSIGNMENT MAY COST YOU EVERYTHING.

━━━━━━➤●◄━━━━━━

Everything important...costs. ALWAYS.

Your salvation was costly. "For ye are bought with a price: therefore glorify God in your body, and in your spirit, which are God's" (1 Corinthians 6:20).

The Assignment of Jesus cost Him social acceptance. "He came unto His own, and His own received Him not" (John 1:11).

The Assignment of Jesus cost Him everything. "Forasmuch as ye know that ye were not redeemed with corruptible things, as silver and gold, from your vain conversation received by tradition from your fathers; But with the precious blood of Christ, as of a lamb without blemish and without spot" (1 Peter 1:18,19).

Jesus even taught His followers that it would be costly for them to follow Him. "Then said Jesus unto his disciples, If any man will come after Me, let him deny himself, and take up his cross, and follow Me. For whosoever will save his life shall lose it: and whosoever will lose his life for My sake shall find it. For what is a man profited, if he shall gain the whole world, and lose his own soul? or what shall a man give in exchange for his soul?" (Matthew 16:24-26).

The Assignment of Moses cost him dearly. "By

faith Moses, when he was come to years, refused to be called the son of Pharaoh's daughter; Choosing rather to suffer affliction with the people of God, than to enjoy the pleasures of sin for a season; Esteeming the reproach of Christ greater riches than the treasures in Egypt: for he had respect unto the recompense of the reward. By faith he forsook Egypt, not fearing the wrath of the king: for he endured, as seeing Him who is invisible" (Hebrews 11:24-27).

The Assignment of Abraham cost him the comfort of his relatives and home. "Now the Lord had said unto Abram, Get thee out of thy country, and from thy kindred, and from thy father's house, unto a land that I will shew thee" (Genesis 12:1). "By faith Abraham, when he was called to go out into a place which he should after receive for an inheritance, obeyed; and he went out, not knowing whither he went. By faith he sojourned in the land of promise, as in a strange country, dwelling in tabernacles with Isaac and Jacob" (Hebrews 11:8,9).

It cost the Apostle Paul his prestige. "Circumcised the eighth day, of the stock of Israel, of the tribe of Benjamin, an Hebrew of the Hebrews; as touching the law, a Pharisee; Concerning zeal, persecuting the church; touching the righteousness which is in the law, blameless. But what things were gain to me, those I counted loss for Christ" (Philippians 3:5-7).

His Assignment cost him physically. "Are they ministers of Christ? (I speak as a fool) I am more; in labours more abundant, in stripes above measure, in prisons more frequent, in deaths oft. Of the Jews five times received I forty stripes save one. Thrice was I beaten with rods, once was I stoned, thrice I suffered shipwreck, a night and a day I have been in the deep; In journeyings often, in perils of waters, in perils of robbers, in perils by mine own countrymen, in perils by the heathen, in perils in the city, in perils in the wilderness, in perils in the sea, in perils among false brethren; In weariness and painfulness, in watchings often, in hunger and thirst, in fastings often, in cold and nakedness. Beside those things that are without, that which cometh upon me daily, the care of all the churches. Who is weak, and I am not weak? who is offended, and I burn not? If I must needs glory, I will glory of the things which concern mine infirmities" (2 Corinthians 11:23-30).

All champions discover the high cost of their Assignment.

The Assignment of Joseph cost him years of slavery, false accusation, and total isolation from his father and family. Esther knew that her Assignment could have cost her very life had the king not accepted her. *Daniel* paid the high cost of enduring the lion's den. *The three Hebrew children* followed their Assignment with total devotion, even through the fiery furnace.

The consecration of Job was not celebrated by his wife. "Then said his wife unto him, Dost thou still retain thine integrity? curse God, and die" (Job 2:9).

Job refused to sin. He stayed true to God.

Payday was coming.

Yes, your Assignment may cost you the highest price you have ever paid for anything in your entire life.

Why should you pay any price to believe your Assignment? *The rewards. They are guaranteed, achievable, and forever.*

Jesus paid the price to produce a future.
"Who for the joy that was set before Him endured the cross, despising the shame, and is set down at the right hand of the throne of God" (Hebrews 12:2).

Here Are 15 Reasons Champions Are Willing To Pay Any Price To Complete Their Assignment:

1.   *The Power Of God Becomes Revealed In Us.*
"But we have this treasure in earthen vessels, that the excellency of the power may be of God, and not of us" (2 Corinthians 4:7).

2.   *The Life Of Jesus Is Made Manifest In Us And To Others.* "Always bearing about in the body the dying of the Lord Jesus, that the life also of Jesus might be made manifest in our body. For we which live are alway delivered unto death for Jesus' sake, that the life also of Jesus might be made manifest in our mortal flesh" (2 Corinthians 4:10,11).

3.   *Your Inner Man Is Renewed Through Daily Adversity.* "For which cause we faint not; but though our outward man perish, yet the inward man is renewed day by day" (2 Corinthians 4:16).

4.   *Many Afflictions Work An Eternal Future Reward From God.* "For our light affliction, which is but for a moment, worketh for us a far more exceeding and eternal weight of glory" (2 Corinthians 4:17).

5.   *Adversity Passes Quickly, But The Rewards Are Forever.* "For our light affliction, which is but for a moment, worketh for us a far more exceeding and

eternal weight of glory; While we look not at the things which are seen, but at the things which are not seen: for the things which are seen are temporal; but the things which are not seen are eternal" (2 Corinthians 4:17,18).

6. *You Must Appear Before The Judgment Seat Of Christ.* "Wherefore we labour, that, whether present or absent, we may be accepted of Him. For we must all appear before the judgment seat of Christ; that everyone may receive the things done in his body, according to that he hath done, whether it be good or bad" (2 Corinthians 5:9,10).

7. *Moses Expected A Reward; So Can We.* "Esteeming the reproach of Christ greater riches than the treasures in Egypt: for he had respect unto the recompense of the reward" (Hebrews 11:26).

8. *A Crown Of Righteousness Awaits.* "I have fought a good fight, I have finished my course, I have kept the faith: Henceforth there is laid up for me a crown of righteousness, which the Lord, the righteous judge, shall give me at that day: and not to me only, but unto all them also that love His appearing" (2 Timothy 4:7,8).

9. *Rulership Follows Adversity.* "If we suffer, we shall also reign with Him" (2 Timothy 2:12).

10. *Refusal To Pay The Price Of Your Assignment Will Alienate You From God.* "If we deny Him, He also will deny us" (2 Timothy 2:12).

11. *Pay The Price Because You Were Chosen To Do So.* "Thou therefore endure hardness, as a good soldier of Jesus Christ. No man that warreth entangleth himself with the affairs of this life; that he may please Him who hath chosen him to be a soldier" (2 Timothy 2:3,4).

12. *Your Joy Is Guaranteed Upon Completion Of Your Assignment, Regardless Of The Cost.* "Beloved, think it not strange concerning the fiery trial which is to try you, as though some strange thing happened unto you: But rejoice, inasmuch as ye are partakers of Christ's sufferings; that, when His glory shall be revealed, ye may be glad also with exceeding joy" (1 Peter 4:12,13).

13. *The Spirit Of Glory Comes And Rests Upon Your Life When You Pay The Price.* "If ye be reproached for the name of Christ, happy are ye; for the spirit of glory and of God resteth upon you" (1 Peter 4:14).

14. *Compensation Is In Every Contract God Made With You.* He does not merely owe you. He simply loves you. He uses rewards as an *incentive for obedience.* "And all these blessings shall come on thee, and overtake thee, if thou shalt hearken unto the voice of the Lord thy God" (Deuteronomy 28:2).

15. *Your Losses Are Temporary; Your Restoration Is Permanent.* "And I will restore to you the years that the locust hath eaten, the cankerworm, and the caterpiller, and the palmerworm, My great army which I sent among you. And ye shall eat in plenty, and be satisfied, and praise the name of the Lord your God, that hath dealt wondrously with you: and My people shall never be ashamed" (Joel 2:25,26).

Payday arrives. You can count on God. Look again at the life of Job. His wife had cursed him. His children had died. His possessions were stolen. His health was gone. But God was not finished blessing him. "And the Lord turned the captivity of Job, when he prayed for his friends: also the Lord gave Job twice as much as he had before. So the Lord blessed the latter end of

Job more than his beginning: for he had fourteen thousand sheep, and six thousand camels, and a thousand yoke of oxen, and a thousand she asses. He had also seven sons and three daughters. And in all the land were no women found so fair as the daughters of Job" (Job 42:10,12,13,15).

It is true. Your Assignment may cost you everything. It may cost you social status, finances, health, and the closest friendships you have built for a lifetime. But a day of reward is guaranteed. *Always.*

One of the greatest preachers in history had a heartbreaking relationship with his wife. She despised his work for God. She would stand in the back of crowds when he ministered, shouting out names at him. But he kept his focus. He refused to respond to her. He only responded to his Assignment and calling. Today most of us would not even know her name, while his ministry has continued to bless thousands to this day.

Refuse to quit. Use patience as a battering ram against opposition. Tomorrow you will taste the rewards of any price you pay today. "Cast not away therefore your confidence, which hath great recompense of reward. For ye have need of patience, that, after ye have done the will of God, ye might receive the promise. For yet a little while, and He that shall come will come, and will not tarry" (Hebrews 10:35-37).

Your payday will not disappoint you.

❧ 18 ❧

YOUR ASSIGNMENT MAY SOMETIMES SEEM TO BE IN VAIN.

Great efforts do not always produce immediate results.

Harvest takes time. Any farmer knows this. He arises early in the morning to sow his Seed. Rains come. The sun beats down. There are hours of toil and days of waiting. Then, the small plants begin to bud. Day after day, the changes occur. Suddenly, it appears his entire land is filled with a bountiful crop. The blessing came after days of toil, sweat, hard labor, time, and money invested—and after a season of waiting...waiting...and more waiting.

The Apostle Paul felt this way. He wrote, "I am afraid of you, lest I have bestowed upon you labour in vain" (Galatians 4:11). He had poured his life out. He had spoken courageously, eloquently, and consistently. Yet, he felt useless at times.

Waiting for changes is proof of your faith.

That kind of faith is what moves the hand of God toward your life. I remember when I first grasped that a mantle of Wisdom was upon my life. It was not my possession of Wisdom, but my *pursuit* of it, that revealed my calling. I had an *obsession* to know the heart and mind of God toward a matter. I shared it with a preacher friend.

"Nobody wants Wisdom, Mike! Everybody wants miracles," was his laughing reply.

Well, I watched it happen before my eyes. Nobody *seemed* to desire Wisdom. Everybody wanted an immediate turnaround miracle touch from God. They would sit for three hours in a service anticipating a miracle, but would not invest $7.00 in a Wisdom book. Most of us want changes without the *seasons* of change.

Ministers often feel useless. They lose confidence in people. Micah, the prophet, often felt that his Assignment was in vain. Here is his assessment of those to whom he was assigned: "The best of them is as a brier: the most upright is sharper than a thorn hedge...trust ye not in a friend" (Micah 7:4,5). Have you ever felt that way? Of course you have. I have, too.

The great king and musician, *David*, once sobbed, "Why art thou cast down, O my soul? and why art thou disquieted within me?" (Psalm 42:11). Yes, the same brave and courageous lad who ran toward Goliath with a slingshot also knew the experience of feeling like his labors were futile.

Jeremiah considered managing a motel in the desert rather than stay in the ministry. "O that I had in the wilderness a lodging place of wayfaring men; that I might leave my people, and go from them!" (Jerermiah 9:2).

Elijah, who could outrun horses and call down fire on water-soaked sacrifices, once hit total despondency. He begged God to kill him. "But he himself went a day's journey into the wilderness, and came and sat down under a juniper tree: and he requested for himself that he might die; and said, It is enough; now, O Lord, take away my life; for I am not better than my fathers" (1 Kings 19:4).

Jesus must have felt at times that His labors were in vain. During the midst of explaining powerful truths to His disciples, Peter, His own disciple, rebuked Him. Jesus had to turn and say, "Get thee behind Me, Satan: thou art an offense unto me: for thou savourest not the things that be of God, but those that be of men" (Matthew 16:23). Imagine having one of the closest prayer partners in your life misunderstand almost everything you say. Jesus must have felt very frustrated at various times with His disciples and others. One day He simply cried out, "O faithless and perverse generation, how long shall I be with you? how long shall I suffer you?" (Matthew 17:17).

Seasons change.

People change.

Your own *needs* and *desires* will change.

Let patience do its work. "Cast not away therefore your confidence, which hath great recompense of reward. For ye have need of patience, that, after ye have done the will of God, ye might receive the promise" (Hebrews 10:35,36).

Never, never, never give up. Your future will always whimper at the feet of Persistence.

❧ 19 ❧

Your Assignment Will Require Miracles.

―――――▸❧◂―――――

Your Assignment will require the supernatural interventions of God.

Jesus said it: "for without Me ye can do nothing" (John 15:5). Your Assignment will require miracles. Miracles require God. And God requires your obedience.

When Joshua and the Israelites approached Jericho, it took a miracle to bring the walls down.

When Gideon and his 300 men took on the huge army of the Midianites, victory required an absolute miracle.

When Naaman dipped in the Jordan River to receive healing of his leprosy, it took a miracle for the healing to occur.

When the wine ran out at the marriage in Cana, it took a miracle of Jesus for the water in the water pots to be turned into wine.

When the widow of Zarephath was eating her last meal, it required a miracle for it to multiply. The Harvest from her Seed fed her, Elijah and her son for the rest of the famine season.

When the armies of Pharaoh chased the Israelites, their drowning in the Red Sea required a miracle.

God never gives you an Assignment that does not require His participation.

So your Assignment will always be *big enough* to require a *miracle*. You will *not* be able to do your Assignment *alone*. You cannot complete your Assignment without the continuous, obvious, and necessary *hand of God*.

You are wanting a *miracle*.

God is wanting a *relationship*.

He makes miracles *necessary* so that you will be motivated to *pursue Him* and His involvement in your life.

God will never involve Himself in a dream that you can achieve alone.

Every single act of God is designed to increase your dependency upon Him and your addiction to Him and His presence. "He humbled thee, and suffered thee to hunger, and fed thee with manna, which thou knewest not, neither did thy fathers know; that He might make thee know that man doth not live by bread only, but by every word that proceedeth out of the mouth of the Lord doth man live" (Deuteronomy 8:3).

Your Father refuses to be forgotten and ignored. "Beware that thou forget not the Lord thy God, in not keeping His commandments, and His judgments, and His statutes, which I command thee this day" (Deuteronomy 8:11).

Your Father permits crisis to inspire memory. "But thou shalt remember the Lord thy God: for it is He that giveth thee power to get wealth, that He may establish His covenant which He sware unto thy fathers, as it is this day" (Deuteronomy 8:18).

Jesus loved performing miracles. "How God

anointed Jesus of Nazareth with the Holy Ghost and with power: Who went about doing good, and healing all that were oppressed of the devil; for God was with Him" (Acts 10:38).

When He talked, each word was an invitation to a miracle. The uncertain are invited to a miracle. The poor are invited to a miracle. "Give, and it shall be given unto you; good measure, pressed down, and shaken together, and running over, shall men give into your bosom. For with the same measure that ye mete withal it shall be measured to you again" (Luke 6:38).

Peter discovered this when Jesus invited him to walk on water. "And Peter answered Him and said, Lord, if it be Thou, bid me come unto Thee on the water. And He said, Come. And when Peter was come down out of the ship, he walked on the water, to go to Jesus" (Matthew 14:28,29). *The sick are invited to a miracle.* The man who had an infirmity for 38 years was invited to a miracle. "When Jesus saw him lie, and knew that he had been now a long time in that case, He saith unto him, Wilt thou be made whole?" (John 5:6).

Here Are 12 Helpful Keys In Unlocking The Flow Of Miracles Into Your Life Assignment:

1.   *Recognize That Any Assignment From God Will Require The Miracles Of God.* You will not succeed alone.

2.   *Expect Miracles In Your Life Daily.* "for he that cometh to God must believe that He is, and that He is a rewarder of them that diligently seek Him" (Hebrews 11:6).

3. *Remember, Miracles Will Require A Continuous Flow Of Your Faith.* "But without faith it is impossible to please Him" (Hebrews 11:6).

4. *Feed Your Faith—Confidence In God.* It enters your heart when you *hear* the words of God *spoken.* "So then faith cometh by hearing, and hearing by the word of God" (Romans 10:17).

5. *Understand That The Logic Of Your Mind And The Faith Of Your Heart Collide.* They will wage war with each other continually throughout your Assignment. "For the flesh lusteth against the Spirit, and the Spirit against the flesh: and these are contrary the one to the other: so that ye cannot do the things that ye would. But the fruit of the Spirit is...faith" (Galatians 5:17,22).

6. *While Logic Produces Order, Faith Will Produce Miracles.* God will never consult your logic to determine your future. He permits your faith to determine the levels of your promotion and victories.

7. *Logic Is The Wonderful And Valuable Gift He Gives You To Create Order In Your Dealings With People.*

8. *Faith Is The Wonderful And Valuable Gift He Gives You To Create Miracles...Through The Father.*

9. *Your Assignment Will Require Miracle Relationships With Mentors, Protégés, Friends, And Connections.* For example, Joseph would never have gotten to the palace without the miracle relationship with the butler, a divine connection.

10. *Your Assignment May Require Supernatural Financial Provision.* For example, Peter experienced the miracle of the coin in the mouth of the fish to pay taxes. Financial miracles are *normal* in the lives of those who obey God.

11. *Your Assignment Will Require The Miracle Of Wisdom.* Your decisions will open doors or close doors. Each decision you make will *increase* you or *decrease* you.

12. *Miracles Come Easily To The Obedient.* "If ye be willing and obedient, ye shall eat the good of the land" (Isaiah 1:19).

Any move toward self-sufficiency is a move away from God. So cultivate continuous gratefulness and thankfulness in your heart for the presence of the Holy Spirit. Check His countenance. Pursue His approval. "The Lord make His face shine upon thee, and be gracious unto thee: the Lord lift up His countenance upon thee, and give thee peace" (Numbers 6:25,26). "Lord, lift Thou up the light of Thy countenance upon us" (Psalm 4:6). His countenance can be a very strong encouragement every moment of your life. "Hope thou in God: for I shall yet praise Him for the help of His countenance" (Psalm 42:5).

Remember: Miracles are coming toward you... or going away from you...every day of your life.

❧ 20 ❧

YOUR ASSIGNMENT WILL REQUIRE YOUR TOTAL FOCUS.

The Only Reason Men Fail Is Broken Focus.

Focus is anything that consumes your time, energy, finances, and attention.

While traveling around the world for more than thirty years and speaking more than 12,000 times, I have listened to the details of personal battles and conflicts of many hurting people. Satan's main goal is to simply break your focus off your Assignment. When he does this, he has mastered you. When he breaks your focus off your Assignment, he has brought pain to the heart of God, Who is his only true enemy.

Jesus encouraged His disciples to keep their focus on the kingdom of God. He assured them that their financial provisions and everything they needed would be produced through absolute *focus upon Him.* "But seek ye *first* the kingdom of God, and His righteousness; and all these things shall be added unto you" (Matthew 6:33).

How important is your focus? Listen to the words of God concerning those who would tempt His people to go to another god. "If thy brother, the son of thy mother, or thy son, or thy daughter, or the wife of thy bosom, or thy friend, which is as thine own soul, entice thee secretly, saying, Let us go and serve other gods, which thou hast not known, thou, nor thy fathers; Namely, of the gods of the people which are round about you, nigh unto thee, or far off from thee, from the one end of the earth even unto the other end of the earth; Thou shalt not consent unto him, nor hearken unto him; neither shall thine eye pity him, neither shalt thou spare, neither shalt thou conceal him: But thou shalt surely kill him; thine hand shall be first upon him to put him to death, and afterwards the hand of all the people. And thou shalt stone him with stones, that he die; because he hath sought to thrust thee away from the Lord thy God, which brought thee out of the land of Egypt, from the house of bondage" (Deuteronomy 13:6-10).

Jesus addressed broken focus in the New Testament. "And if thy right eye offend thee, pluck it out, and cast it from thee: for it is profitable for thee that one of thy members should perish, and not that thy whole body should be cast into hell. And if thy right hand offend thee, cut it off, and cast it from thee: for it is profitable for thee that one of thy members should perish, and not that thy whole body should be cast into hell" (Matthew 5:29,30).

How do you destroy someone's goal? Give him another one. How do you destroy a dream in someone? Give him another dream. It *fragments his focus*. It *dilutes his energy*.

Here Are 12 Wisdom Principles On Focus That Can Make A Real Difference In Your Life:

1. *Focus Determines Mastery. Anything that has the ability to keep your attention has mastered you.* Any significant progress toward the completion of your Assignment will require your every thought, your every cent, every hour of your life.

2. *Your Focus Determines Your Energy.* Think for a moment. Let us say you are sleepy, laid back on your pillows. The television is on. Suddenly, the telephone rings. Someone in your family has just had a crisis. They are being rushed to the hospital. Do you go back to sleep easily? Of course not. Your focus has changed. Suddenly, you have leaped to your feet. You put on your clothes, jump in your car, and head down to the hospital. *Focus* determines your *energy*.

3. *What You Look At The Longest Becomes The Strongest In Your Life.* The Apostle Paul focused on his future. "Brethren, I count not myself to have apprehended: but this one thing I do, forgetting those things which are behind, and reaching forth unto those things which are before, I press toward the mark for the prize of the high calling of God in Christ Jesus" (Philippians 3:13,14).

4. *Broken Focus Creates Insecurity And Instability In Everything Around You.* "A double minded man is unstable in all his ways" (James 1:8).

5. *Only Focused Faith Can Produce Miracles From The Hand Of God.* "But let him ask in faith, nothing wavering. For he that wavereth is like a wave of the sea driven with the wind and tossed. For let not

that man think that he shall receive anything of the Lord" (James 1:6,7).

6. *Sight Affects Desire.* What you keep looking upon, you eventually pursue. "Mine eye affecteth mine heart" (Lamentations 3:51). Joshua, the remarkable leader of the Israelites, wrote this instruction from God. "Only be thou strong and very courageous, that thou mayest observe to do according to all the law, which Moses My servant commanded thee: turn not from it to the right hand or to the left, that thou mayest prosper whithersoever thou goest. This book of the law shall not depart out of thy mouth; but thou shalt meditate therein day and night, that thou mayest observe to do according to all that is written therein: for then thou shalt make thy way prosperous, and then thou shalt have good success" (Joshua 1:7,8).

7. *Focusing On The Word Of God Daily Is Necessary To Complete Your Assignment Properly.* God instructed the people of Israel to teach, train, and mentor their children on His words. Listen to this incredible instruction: "Therefore shall ye lay up these My words in your heart and in your soul, and bind them for a sign upon your hand, that they may be as frontlets between your eyes. And ye shall teach them your children, speaking of them when thou sittest in thine house, and when thou walkest by the way, when thou liest down, and when thou risest up. And thou shalt write them upon the door posts of thine house, and upon thy gates" (Deuteronomy 11:18-20).

8. *Focusing, Hearing, And Speaking The Word Of God Continually Makes You Invincible.* "There shall no man be able to stand before you: for the Lord your God shall lay the fear of you and the

dread of you upon all the land that ye shall tread upon, as He hath said unto you" (Deuteronomy 11:25). This is one of the reasons I keep cassettes of the Word of God in every room of my home. The first thing I do daily is turn on my tape player and listen to Scriptures being read. It washes my mind, purges my heart, and harnesses my focus.

9. *Focus Has Reward.* "That your days may be multiplied, and the days of your children, in the land which the Lord sware unto your fathers to give them, as the days of heaven upon the earth. For if ye shall diligently keep all these commandments which I command you, to do them, to love the Lord your God, to walk in all His ways, and to cleave unto Him; Then will the Lord drive out all these nations from before you, and ye shall possess greater nations and mightier than yourselves. Every place whereon the soles of your feet shall tread shall be yours" (Deuteronomy 11:21-24).

10. *What You Keep Seeing Determines Your Focus.* "I will set no wicked thing before mine eyes: I hate the work of them that turn aside; it shall not cleave to me" (Psalm 101:3).

11. *Your Enemy Is Anyone Who Breaks Your Focus From A God-Given Assignment.*

12. *Your Friend Is Anyone Who Helps Keep You Focused On The Instructions Of God For Your Life.*

Here Are Six Keys To Protecting Your Focus:

1. *Recognize That Broken Focus Destroys Your Dreams.* It creates an unending parade of tragedies and disasters in your life.

2. *Take Personal Responsibility.* Be the gatekeeper for your eyes, ears, and heart. Nobody else can fully protect you. You must be protected by God, *as you yield yourself to Him.*

3. *Control The Music And Teaching That Enter Your Ears.* What you hear determines what you *feel.* "And all Israel shall hear, and fear, and shall do no more any such wickedness as this is among you" (Deuteronomy 13:11). What you hear determines what you *fear.*

4. *Keep Continuous Praise On Your Lips* And Throughout Your Home. I keep music playing 24 hours a day on my property and in my home. Every room in my house has sound and every minute there is music to the Holy Spirit being sung and played. I have 24 speakers on the trees in my seven-acre yard. I am determined to *protect my focus.*

5. *Starve Wrong Friendships.* Wrong friends do not feed, fuel, and fertilize your total focus on your Assignment. Let those friendships die. Samson did not have to date everyone to get his hair cut. *He only required one wrong person to destroy his future.*

6. *Pursue And Permit Only Relationships That Increase Your Focus On Your Assignment.*

It was late one night in southern Florida. The service had ended. Several preachers wanted to go to a restaurant. As I sat there, I listened to the conversation. (I have two major interests in my life:

learning and teaching. Both must take place continually for me to have pleasure!) I listened as everyone discussed ball games, politics, and tragedies. I kept listening for worthy Wisdom Keys that might be imparted; I listened for important questions that might be asked. Neither took place. Several times I attempted to change the direction of the conversation, but it seemed ignored. I was too tired to dominate and take charge, too weary to force the conversation in an appropriate direction.

The Holy Spirit was *not* the focus.

So I quietly stood and said, "I must leave. God bless each of you." I left. I wish I could have that kind of courage every *year* of my lifetime, every *day* of my lifetime!

Focus is the Master Key to the Golden Door of Success.

∼ 21 ∼

You Must Only Attempt A God-Given And God-Approved Assignment.

God will never sustain what He has not birthed. Ideas are options. *Commands* from God are *not.* Your imagination can produce a thousand ideas, options, or alternatives. When God speaks, His instructions are not to be altered, ignored, or refuted.

You will often hear someone talk about a "God-idea." Obviously, this is intended to convey the thought that God would inspire an invention or new method for doing something. It is based on Proverbs 8:12, "I Wisdom dwell with prudence, and find out knowledge of witty inventions." Yes, God inspires many wonderful improvements and corrections in our lives. In reality, a thought or idea is not necessarily a command.

However, if you study the Bible carefully, there is no record in Scripture of where God gave someone an idea. He gives *instructions.* He gives *commands.*

There were occasions when someone sinned, and God let them choose the type of judgment they could experience. It happened in the life of David, after his sin. When he numbered Israel, it displeased the Lord. "And David said unto God, I have sinned greatly, because I have done this thing: but now, I beseech Thee, do away the iniquity of thy servant; for I have done very foolishly" (1 Chronicles 21:8).

When God spoke to the prophet Gad, He told Gad to "Go and tell David, saying, Thus saith the Lord, I offer thee three things: choose thee one of them, that I may do it unto thee" (1 Chronicles 21:10). David replied, "let me fall now into the hand of the Lord; for very great are His mercies: but let me not fall into the hand of man" (1 Chronicles 21:13).

It is very important that you do not attempt to achieve a dream or a goal that God did not instruct you to pursue. Wrong goals will become substitutes for the right goals. Wrong dreams become substitutes for the right dreams. And when you pursue something God did not intend you to have, He is not obligated to sustain you, emotionally, physically, or financially.

Anything you pursue alone will fail.

After David had conquered his enemies, he was sitting in his house. He indicated to Nathan, the prophet, that he wanted to build a special house for God. The prophet immediately responded, "Go, do all that is in thine heart; for the Lord is with thee" (2 Samuel 7:3). (Even prophets can be wrong when they fail to consult God.)

That evening God spoke to Nathan to bring a special word to David. David was *not* to build the house of the Lord. Rather, God had established that His Seed would do so instead. "I will set up thy Seed after thee, which shall proceed out of thy bowels, and I will establish his kingdom. He shall build an house for

My name" (2 Samuel 7:12,13).

Solomon was the son who built the temple. "And Solomon sent to Hiram, saying, Thou knowest how that David my father could not build an house unto the name of the Lord his God for the wars which were about him on every side, until the Lord put them under the soles of his feet. But now the Lord my God hath given me rest on every side, so that there is neither adversary nor evil occurrent. And, behold, I purpose to build an house unto the name of the Lord my God, as the Lord spake unto David my father, saying, Thy son, whom I will set upon thy throne in thy room, he shall build an house unto my name" (1 Kings 5:2-5). *Mentors often see the future of their protégés years in advance.*

An idea is not a command from God. You will have many wonderful and inspired ideas throughout your lifetime. When God is involved, it will not be simply an idea: It will be an instruction and a command.

I have pursued several projects throughout my lifetime that God did not put His hand upon. They exhausted me emotionally, physically, spiritually, and financially. Looking back across the pages of my achievements, I wish I had waited for a *direct command from the Holy Spirit* on each project.

Why do we pursue wrong projects? For several reasons. I talked recently to a minister who had invested millions of dollars in a hotel. His congregation and partners had urged him to do so in order to be close to his ministry and services. God did not instruct him to do so. *The needs of the people motivated him instead of the voice of the Holy Spirit.*

It is easy to be stirred and motivated by the needs of those close to you instead of by the voice of God. When you do so, you bring disasters and heartache into your life. *So, the needs of others are not necessarily commands from God.*

Sometimes, our own boredom with the same routine inspires us to *try something different.* One of the greatest evangelists in our generation once told me, "Mike, the biggest mistake of my life was when I got tired of doing the same thing over and over. I decided I wanted to see something change. It was the biggest mistake of my ministry. I lost hundreds of thousands of partners and support. I simply missed God."

One of my great mentors once told me, "When you get sick and tired of saying something, you are just then *beginning* to get it yourself. When your staff gets sick and tired of hearing you say something, they are just then *beginning* to get it. When your people get sick and tired of hearing you teach something, they are just then *beginning to understand it.*"

Fight against boredom by returning to His presence for fresh inspiration and any new instructions. *Do not permit your imagination to become your guide in scheduling your Assignment.*

Recently, I was escorted through a multimillion-dollar addition to a church. I spoke to the pastor, "This is wonderful!" I knew that he had taught for several years that it was wrong to borrow money. He paid cash every step of the way. So, I continued my expression of admiration.

"Just think. You will have all of this paid for step by step in cash."

He looked a little sheepish. "Well, I have been so excited about this project that I decided to borrow the money. I have never believed in doing that, but I really wanted to see this project take place. And the bank was more than willing to loan it to us."

I could not believe what I was hearing. He had taught and written in his books that it was wrong to borrow money. But now he was doing so. He was borrowing more than a million dollars from the bank in direct contradiction to his entire teaching. So I asked him, "Did the Holy Spirit command you to build this *right now?*"

He looked as though I had slapped him across his face. "Well no, I cannot say that God commanded me to do this. But our church would love to have a gymnasium, and a new cafeteria and all these facilities. We need them. It must be God, or the bank would not have loaned us the money."

Well, banks *loan money. That is their job.* They make money doing so. Why should we consider a loan from a bank to be *a miracle?* It is absurd logic. Actually, it is not logical at all. *Attempt only those things which are commanded by the Holy Spirit for your life.*

Provision is only guaranteed at the place of obedience.

When I have invested *time* in The Secret Place to receive confirmation and reassurance concerning the will of God, the *inner peace has sustained me* in crises and difficult places that occur; knowing that "If God be for us, who can be against us?" (Romans 8:31).

Any worthwhile Assignment creates enemies. It is vital that you know *beyond any doubt* that God will be an enemy to your enemies, a friend to your friends, and will walk with you through the completion of any instruction.

Another reason we attempt projects that God did not inspire is *salesmanship*. Someone who is articulate and persuasive convinces us that something is the "chance of a lifetime. You had better do it now, or it will be your last opportunity forever." *Nothing is more plentiful than opportunities.* The universe is crammed with millions of opportunities.

You will never lack for an opportunity. It is your ability to *focus* and give your best effort to any opportunity that makes the difference.

How much influence has God had in your past decisions? How much private time have you invested in The Secret Place regarding a project?

When I stay in The Secret Place (my private prayer room dedicated to the Holy Spirit) my conclusions are always different from those of advisors. *God sees further ahead than anyone.* He is swift to convey His answers when pursued. "Except the Lord build the house, they labour in vain that build it" (Psalm 127:1). I believe it. Keep listening for the voice of the Holy Spirit. He will speak when His opinion is *respected, treasured, and pursued.*

"I am leaving the evangelistic field and birthing a new church," said a young minister several months ago.

"So, God has commanded you to become a pastor?" I asked.

"Not really, but my wife is tired of my traveling. I have two children that I need to raise. It is the only thing I can do right now."

"You are going to birth a church *without the command and instruction of the Holy Spirit?*" I asked incredulously.

He hung his head. He stared ahead for a few moments. He could not answer. We have become so accustomed to creating and designing our own blueprints for our lives that the Holy Spirit is being consulted these days only in crisis situations. It is quite possible that the crisis would not arrive at all had He been consulted first.

Nobody else is responsible for your Assignment but you.

⚒ 22 ⚒

YOU WILL ONLY SUCCEED WHEN YOUR ASSIGNMENT BECOMES AN OBSESSION.

———————⟶⟩●◁⟵———————

Focus is magnetic.

When you give your attention, time, and total effort to achieving your Assignment, you will experience extraordinary currents of favor and miracles. *As I have written, whatever has the ability to keep your attention, has mastered you.*

Jesus Himself rebuked those who attempted to break His focus and obsession for completing the will of the Father. "But when He had turned about and looked on His disciples, He rebuked Peter, saying, Get thee behind Me, Satan: for thou savourest not the things that be of God, but the things that be of men" (Mark 8:33).

The Apostle Paul was obsessed with his Assignment. That explains his remarkable success in the face of enemies, adversaries, and even friends who misunderstood him. It explains his letter to the Philippians, "this one thing I do, forgetting those things which are behind, and reaching forth unto those things which are before, I press toward the mark for the prize of the high calling of God in Christ Jesus" (Philippians 3:13,14).

He moved *away* from past hurts, failures, and memories. Obviously, he had a *photograph* of those things God had placed before him.

The Apostle Paul Understood The Five Keys To Developing An Obsession For Your Assignment:

1. *Refuse Any Weight Or Distraction To Your Assignment.* "let us lay aside every weight, and the sin which doth so easily beset us, and let us run with patience the race that is set before us" (Hebrews 12:1).

2. *Be Ruthless In Severing Any Ties To A Project Not Connected To Your Assignment.* He instructed Timothy, "No man that warreth entangleth himself with the affairs of this life; that he may please Him who hath chosen him to be a soldier" (2 Timothy 2:4).

3. *Constantly Study Your Assignment.* He urged Timothy, "Study to shew thyself approved unto God, a workman that needeth not to be ashamed, rightly dividing the word of truth" (2 Timothy 2:15).

4. *Shun Conversations That Are Unrelated To Your Assignment.* "But shun profane and vain babblings: for they will increase unto more ungodliness. But foolish and unlearned questions avoid, knowing that they do gender strifes" (2 Timothy 2:16,23).

5. *Learn To Disconnect From Any Relationship That Does Not Feed Your Addiction To His Presence And Your Obsession To Complete God's Assignment In Your Life.* "And if any man obey not our word by this epistle, note that man, and have no company with him,

that he may be ashamed" (2 Thessalonians 3:14).
Satan dreads the *completion* of your Assignment.
Each act of obedience can destroy a thousand satanic
plans and desires.

I must share with you an experience. You will
appreciate it because I am certain it will happen to
you in your future (if it has not already happened).
My secretary handed me the telephone number of a
friend I had known 25 years ago. He had not written
me for 25 years. He had not telephoned me for 25 years.
He had not sown a Seed in my ministry for 25 years.
Suddenly, he telephoned several times. He came to
my weekly Bible study. He sowed a generous Seed in
my ministry. He wanted to have supper.

"Mike, I am making more than $20,000 a month.
It is the most wonderful company I have ever been
involved with. I want you to become a part of it with
me."

"Well," I replied slowly, "I am very consumed with
my ministry. I really do not have the time to develop
a secondary income at this point in my life. But, I
appreciate it."

He was stunned. "But I know that you will need
a strong financial base when you retire in the future.
It is easy. You know thousands of people. You do not
have to do anything but ask me to come and present
this multi-level marketing plan to your people. They
will come because they know you personally. And, this
product is the best on the market. People will always
need this product. Your people *need* them."

Well, I was impressed with his $20,000 per month
income, but I had to be very direct with him. "I like

your product. I believe everyone should have one. I will buy one from you. I will tell my friends about you, but I cannot get involved in selling them, because this product cannot consume my attention, efforts, and time. It would be impossible for me to develop an obsession with this product. You see, I know that *I can only succeed with something that consumes and envelopes me.* Besides that, I have not had an instruction from the Lord to pursue a business with this product."

My instructions had already arrived. *My inner peace was proof I was in the center of my Assignment.* Yet, there will always be others who will have wonderful ideas and will offer you options other than your Assignment. Any hours you spend with them is a waste of their time and yours. *I never heard from this man again.*

You see, he had no interest in my Assignment whatsoever. He was only interested in my involvement *with his dream.* I was merely *a vehicle to generate finances* back into his own life.

My secretary handed me another telephone message recently. It was from a dear friend of mine who is well known in ministry circles. He had built an incredible work for God, but due to extreme adversity had experienced some major losses in his personal life and in his ministry. I returned the telephone call.

"Mike, we have got to get together soon."

"Great! When do you want to meet?"

"Could you meet me tonight?" was his reply.

I could not imagine why this man wanted to meet with me so urgently. He had not telephoned me two times in the previous eight years. Suddenly, it was life and death. We met and talked. He was involved in a multi-level marketing program. He would succeed and I knew that. I also realized that anyone linked to him would have significant success. He is a remarkable, brilliant, and enjoyable friend. But he had a *different focus*. I was very direct. "I really believe you could succeed significantly in this business. But, do you feel that this would distract you from the calling of God for ministry?"

"Oh, I will continue to have my ministry, but this will help people financially everywhere."

"I will pray about it, of course. But, my obsession has become the Holy Spirit and spending time in The Secret Place. I have known more peace and joy since building my days around His presence than I have ever known in my lifetime. Financial freedom is wonderful, but doing the will of God and being in the center of my Assignment has become my obsession," I replied carefully.

I have not heard from him again.

When you insist on building your life around your Assignment, wrong relationships will die. Right relationships will be born. I have said it a thousand times: The best way to disconnect from wrong people is to become obsessed with doing the right thing.

When your obsession is to do the right thing, wrong people will find you unbearable.

It is permissible for others to share their dreams. But it is disappointing to discover that they want nothing to do with you nor your Assignment. It is rewarding to know that the Father will reward you one hundredfold for *your obsession* to do His plan. (Read Mark 10:28-30.)

Fight for your focus. Battle hard. Build walls that strengthen your concentration. Ignore the jeers, laughter, and criticism that you are "obsessed."

Those who are obsessed with their Assignment rule this planet called earth.

∞ 23 ∞

YOUR ASSIGNMENT REQUIRES PLANNING.

Planning is often burdensome.

I dislike planning. It seems to take the spontaneity out of life! I am quite creative. My friends know that I like to move suddenly. Now, I think about things long before I do them. But I like to keep them in my mind. It is difficult, tedious, and laborious to move my thoughts toward paper and allow my circle of counsel to analyze, evaluate, and even criticize my goals. However, it is one of the common denominators of champions—they think *ahead*.

Recently, I read where the Chief Executive Officer of 200 corporations invested the first one hour of each day in meticulous planning of that 24-hour day. I have never known anyone personally who has spent that kind of time carefully *planning a day*. This man writes out his plans in detail on paper.

Lee Iacocca, the legendary former head of Chrysler, said that one of his greatest mentors insisted that any ideas he had be written out in detail on paper before he would consider them.

You see, anyone can get carried away in the climate of conversation. But when you are *required to write out a detailed plan on paper,* facts arise that were previously hidden. *Truths* are much easier to see. *Problem* areas emerge. *Weaknesses* become obvious. Anything cloudy becomes clear. *Questions* are answered.

That is why the Scriptures teach, "Write the vision, and make it plain upon tables, that he may run that readeth it" (Habakkuk 2:2). You see, *your Bible is a collection of plans.* God wanted you to see, observe, meditate upon, and visualize those plans.

The Bible is a collection of champions who planned their successes ahead of time. Solomon had a plan for the *temple.* It was quite detailed. (Read the third and fourth Chapters of 2 Chronicles.) Noah had a plan for the *ark.* (See Genesis 6:14-16.) Moses had a plan for the *tabernacle.* (Read Chapters 36-40 in Exodus.)

God even had detailed plans regarding *offerings from the people!* (Read Chapters 1-9 in Leviticus.)

Four Rewards Of Planning:

1. *Planning Ahead Eliminates Stress In Difficult Seasons Of Your Life.* "Go to the ant, thou sluggard; consider her ways, and be wise: Which having no guide, overseer, or ruler, Provideth her meat in the summer, and gathereth her food in the Harvest" (Proverbs 6:6-8).

2. *Planning Greatly Effects The Decisions You Make.* "Or what king, going to make war against another king, sitteth not down first, and consulteth whether he be able with ten thousand to meet him that cometh against him with twenty thousand? Or else, while the other is yet a great way off, he sendeth an ambassage, and desireth conditions of peace" (Luke 14:31,32).

3. *The Quality Of Your Preparation Determines*

The Quality Of Your Performance. "Seest thou a man diligent in his business? he shall stand before kings; he shall not stand before mean men" (Proverbs 22:29). Great concert pianists invest many hours in practice before their concerts. The crowds hear only the results of their preparation.

4. *Proper Planning Guarantees Completion Of Any Project.* "For which of you, intending to build a tower, sitteth not down first, and counteth the cost, whether he have sufficient to finish it? Lest haply, after he hath laid the foundation, and is not able to finish it, all that behold it begin to mock him, Saying, This man began to build, and was not able to finish" (Luke 14:28-30).

The heavyweight boxing champions plan many weeks *before* they will fight. *They prepare.* They know it is the only difference between winning and losing. I have often said that champions do not *become* champions in the ring. They are recognized in the ring. *Their becoming champions occurred in their daily routine.*

It seems that most of us have a dominant influence of either our mind or our heart. There are Mind People and Heart People. Mind People are methodical, analytical, and make decisions based on facts. Heart People appear more sensitive, more intuitive, and they lean toward spontaneity and flexibility.

Mind People desire *facts.*

Heart People desire *inspiration.*

Both kinds of people are necessary in completing your life Assignment. It is my personal observation that *Mind People* often drift away from The Secret

Place, developing a dependence upon their academic studies and gathered data. *Heart People* often move away from mentorship and written discoveries of others, toward special revelation in their prayer time.

Two Important Principles Have Helped Me Greatly:

▶ *Praying* does not replace *planning.*
▶ *Planning* cannot replace *praying.*

Let me illustrate. Study Joshua and the two battles of Ai in Joshua 7. Joshua did not consult the Lord, and lost the first battle of Ai. It devastated him. "And Joshua rent his clothes, and fell to the earth upon his face before the ark of the Lord until the eventide, he and the elders of Israel, and put dust upon their heads" (Joshua 7:6).

Now Israel had sinned. They had taken of the accursed things. In the defeat, God was judging them. God instructed Joshua to quit praying. "Get thee up; wherefore liest thou thus upon thy face?" (Joshua 7:10). It is one of the few times that God did not respond to prayer. *God's plan had not been pursued. It was ignored. Obviously, an entire day of prayer could not replace the simplicity of the plan of God.* "Behold, to obey is better than sacrifice, and to hearken than the fat of rams" (1 Samuel 15:22).

After the sin of Achan was revealed and *penalized,* God spoke *again.* Joshua was listening this time. God promised victory, but stressed again the importance of *following a plan.* "only the spoil thereof, and the cattle thereof, shall ye take for a prey unto yourselves: *lay thee an ambush* for the city *behind* it" (Joshua 8:2).

As the next verses reveal, Joshua had a meticulous plan, and won the second battle of Ai. Praying did not replace his planning. *Praying revealed the plan of God.*

The Seven Most Important Keys In Planning Are:

1. *Ask God For Wisdom.* (See James 1:5.)
2. *Keep A Daily Planner, A Time Management System.* You can find them in office supply stores, or you may secure a recommendation on one by someone you admire.
3. *Keep It Handy, And Refer To It Often.* Using a planner is quite difficult at first and may even seem to slow you down. But it will prove to be a valuable and necessary tool for long-term gain in your life.
4. *Write It Out In Detail.*
5. *Follow It On A Daily Basis.*
6. *Develop A Detailed Picture Of Your Desired End And Conclusion.*
7. *Keep Flexible For The Unexpected, And Adapt The Plan Accordingly.* It takes a *moment* to get a *command* from God. It takes your *lifetime* to get the *plan* from God.

I am learning to stay in The Secret Place past the moment of hearing a command from the Lord. When I linger in His presence, He begins to show me the plans for achieving and accomplishing those commands that He has imparted.

Noah heard in a moment, "Build an ark." But, he had to linger longer to hear the details of building a safe ark and the plan for the inhabitants of it.

Three Powerful Ingredients Produce A Successful Plan. Your Planning Should Begin With:

1. *Time In The Secret Place.* "He that dwelleth in the secret place of the most High shall abide under the shadow of the Almighty" (Psalm 91:1).

Your Time In The Secret Place Determines Your Strength In The Public Place. "But they that wait upon the Lord shall renew their strength; they shall mount up with wings as eagles; they shall run, and not be weary; and they shall walk, and not faint" (Isaiah 40:31).

2. *Your Planning Should Involve Your Circle Of Counsel.* "Two are better than one; because they have a good reward for their labour" (Ecclesiastes 4:9).

Worthy advisors keep you safe from mistakes. "Where no counsel is, the people fall: but in the multitude of counsellors there is safety" (Proverbs 11:14).

David, though he was wise himself, knew how to tap into the mental capability and anointing of others. "And of the children of Issachar, which were men that had *understanding of the times, to know what Israel ought to do;* the heads of them were two hundred; and all their brethren were at their commandment" (1 Chronicles 12:32).

3. *Your Planning Should Involve The Constant Consulting Of Your Lifetime Mentor, The Holy Spirit.* "But the Comforter, which is the Holy Ghost, whom the Father will send in My name, He shall teach you

all things, and bring all things to your remembrance, whatsoever I have said unto you" (John 14:26).

A closing note: Think about it. The Marriage Supper of the Lamb has been planned for more than six thousand years now. Just imagine the splendor, the majesty, and the memory it will create!

The more thorough the plan, the longer your memory of the event will be.

❧ 24 ❧

YOUR ASSIGNMENT WILL BE REVEALED PROGRESSIVELY.

———————

Your puzzle is revealed piece by piece.

You will not receive an understanding of your entire Assignment during one visit with God. He is interested in a relationship, not an event. He requires *continuous exchange* with Him. He imparts information a paragraph at a time, not a chapter at a time. "But the word of the Lord was unto them precept upon precept, precept upon precept; line upon line, line upon line; here a little, and there a little" (Isaiah 28:13).

Each day produces *new clues* to your Assignment. Philip experienced his instructions from the Holy Spirit piece by piece. First, "The angel of the Lord spake unto Philip, saying, Arise, and go toward the south unto the way that goeth down from Jerusalem unto Gaza, which is desert" (Acts 8:26).

So he went. When he arrived, he noticed a eunuch sitting in a chariot. This Ethiopian, the treasurer for Candace the queen of the Ethiopians, was reading Isaiah. Then, another instruction came.

"Then the Spirit said unto Philip, Go near, and join thyself to this chariot" (Acts 8:29).

Then after the eunuch was baptized, Philip received another instruction and "Philip was found at Azotus: and passing through he preached in all the cities, till he came to Caesarea" (Acts 8:40). What you do first determines what God reveals next. When I was a young minister, I wanted God to give me a total photograph of the journey and the conclusion. I fasted for it. I prayed for it. I pursued the observations of worthy mentors. But, it never happened. Somebody has called it, "One day at a time." It takes *hourly dependency* upon the Holy Spirit to develop the relationship that He desires between you and Him.

Moses understood this principle very well. True, it became discouraging at times, but it kept him linked to God and dependent upon Him. Moses watched each plague, from dying fish, frogs, lice and flies, death of cattle and hail mixed with fire, to swarms of locust, like a collection of seasons. (See Exodus Chapters 7-10.)

The smallest instruction has a purpose. You will not always understand it. You may wish and pray for more. But His method of measuring out instructions is to *increase your faith step by step.* It is similar to a weight trainer who carefully and patiently works a young man from lifting 50 pounds on the bench press to eventually lifting 150 pounds. Had he demanded and required the full weight at the beginning, the young man would have become demoralized, discouraged, and depressed. He would have quit.

But the trainer places just enough stress and expectation to grow small levels of strength, confidence, and expectation. Remember this Wisdom Key: You Can Go Anywhere You Want To Go If You Are Willing To Take Enough Small Steps.

Instructions are seasonal. That is why God used the cloud and the fire to guide Moses. "thy cloud standeth over them, and that thou goest before them, by day time in a pillar of a cloud, and in a pillar of fire by night" (Numbers 14:14).

Receiving instructions from the Holy Spirit reminds me much of the gathering of the manna by the Israelites. *Each morning required fresh pursuit.* Only on the sixth day did He provide extra to store for the Sabbath. He wanted them to stay in a *continuous attitude of thanksgiving.* He desired total addiction to His presence and awareness of His importance. *Every morning you must enter the Secret Place for fresh instructions* for that very day. In my own personal life, it has been impossible to gather up a stack of instructions for the years ahead! He requires continuous pursuit.

What you do first determines what God will do second. When I complete His first instruction, I become qualified for His second instruction. "But seek ye first the kingdom of God, and his righteousness; and all these things shall be added unto you" (Matthew 6:33).

Keep listening for His voice. The Holy Spirit is talking to you. "And thine ears shall hear a word behind thee, saying, This is the way, walk ye in it, when ye turn to the right hand, and when ye turn to the left" (Isaiah 30:21).

You will never progress beyond your last point of disobedience.

❧ 25 ❧

Intercessors Can Determine The Outcome Of Your Assignment.

God always responds to pursuit.

Intercession is pursuit of God. I am thrilled over the awakening in the body of Christ to the prayer life, the prayer place, "The Secret Place."

When God is ignored, failure is inevitable. When God is pursued, success is inevitable.

God will not permit your success without Him.

Review These Seven Examples Of Champions Who Understood The Power Of Intercession, Praying Together For Miracles:

1. *Peter Had The Power Of Intercession.* Peter was a powerful man of God. He had walked beside Jesus for three-and-a-half years. He had experienced personal failure and restoration. He had revelation that few men had. "And Jesus answered and said unto him, Blessed art thou, Simon Barjona: for flesh and blood hath not revealed it unto thee, but My Father which is in heaven. And I say also unto thee, That thou art Peter, and upon this rock I will build my

church; and the gates of hell shall not prevail against it. And I will give unto thee the keys of the kingdom of heaven: and whatsoever thou shalt bind on earth shall be bound in heaven: and whatsoever thou shalt loose on earth shall be loosed in heaven" (Matthew 16:17-19).

Yet he was kept in prison. *He needed intercessors.* He needed *others.* Read Acts 12:5: "Peter therefore was kept in prison: but prayer was made without ceasing of the church unto God for him." God sent an angel and released him from prison, *because intercessors prayed.*

2.   *The Prophet Samuel Was An Intercessor.* He made a powerful statement: "Moreover as for me, God forbid that I should sin against the Lord in ceasing to pray for you" (1 Samuel 12:23). He felt that *prayerlessness was sin.* Prayer is the only real proof of humility, recognizing our need for God.

3.   *The Apostle Paul Believed In Intercession,* Praying For Others. Paul had a brilliant mind. He knew Scripture. He knew the Word of God. He had remarkable revelation. Yet he wrote to his protégé, Timothy, concerning his prayer life and intercession: "I thank God, whom I serve from my forefathers with pure conscience, that without ceasing I have remembrance of thee in my prayers night and day" (2 Timothy 1:3).

4.   *Jesus Prayed All Night.* "And it came to pass in those days, that He went out into a mountain   to pray, and continued all night in prayer to God" (Luke 6:12). When you read the context of this verse, you see that He was under great attack. It was the next day when He chose His twelve disciples. So Jesus

invested hours in intercession during battle seasons and during times of decision making.

5. *Jesus Is Interceding For You In Heaven.* "It is Christ that died, yea rather, that is risen again, who is even at the right hand of God, who also maketh intercession for us" (Romans 8:34).

6. *The Holy Spirit Is Interceding For You On Earth.* "Likewise the Spirit also helpeth our infirmities: for we know not what we should pray for as we ought: but the Spirit itself maketh intercession for us with groanings which cannot be uttered. And He that searcheth the hearts knoweth what is the mind of the Spirit, because He maketh intercession for the saints according to the will of God" (Romans 8:26,27).

7. *The Assignment Of Peter Was Protected By The Prayers Of Jesus.* "And the Lord said, Simon, Simon, behold, Satan hath desired to have you, that he may sift you as wheat: But I have prayed for thee, that thy faith fail not: and when thou art converted, strengthen thy brethren" (Luke 22:31,32).

As you read that verse, it becomes clear that Jesus knew Peter's enemy, yet He believed that Peter's faith would not fail because of His prayers for him, He expected His intercession to produce a Harvest. Peter would strengthen the brethren because of his own answered prayers.

Here Are Eight Wisdom Keys To Remember About Intercession:

1. *Beauty, Talent, And Favor Are Not Enough To Create A Successful Assignment.* Esther knew this. She was the most beautiful woman in 127 provinces, yet did not depend on her physical beauty for answers.

She called a fast. "Go, gather together all the Jews that are present in Shushan, and fast ye for me, and neither eat nor drink three days, night or day: I also and my maidens will fast likewise; and so will I go in unto the king, which is not according to the law: and if I perish, I perish" (Esther 4:16).

2. *Intercession Will Produce What Relationships Cannot.* Esther did not depend on her relationship with the king to achieve a successful Assignment. She knew she needed the supernatural intervention of God.

3. *Intercession Is Not A Substitute For Labor And Productivity.* Rather, it causes your *efforts to be productive.* Let me explain. When Esther called a fast, it was not to enable her to avoid facing the king. Her intercession was to *influence the favor of man toward her work.* She linked with God, expecting God to go ahead of her and make her efforts successful.

4. *Intercession Is Not An Invitation To Idleness And Sluggishness.* Intercession will not birth non-involvement. It is the securing of God's involvement with your life.

5. *Never Pray For Anything You Can Doubt.* If I do not have a Scriptural basis for a petition, I refuse to pray it. It keeps my prayers pure, accurate, and in accordance with the will of God.

6. *Learn To Respect The Intercessors God Has Already Linked To Your Life.* "Again I say unto you, That if two of you shall agree on earth as touching any thing that they shall ask, it shall be done for them of my Father which is in heaven" (Matthew 18:19). I take prayer requests very seriously. You see, most people do not really believe in intercession. Most

do not believe that prayer really works. I have sent thousands of prayer request forms to friends and partners, and yet I often receive only a small fraction of them in return.

Does this indicate that they are all experiencing perfect success in their lives and do not need prayer? Of course not. *They simply do not believe that the prayers of a man of God truly work.* "The effectual fervent prayer of a righteous man availeth much" (James 5:16).

7. *Keep Your Circle Of Intercessors Informed.* You see, even God requires that you make known your needs to Him *before He will involve Himself.* "Be careful for nothing; but in every thing by prayer and supplication with thanksgiving let your requests be made known unto God" (Philippians 4:6).

James instructed, "Is any sick among you? let him call for the elders of the church; and let them pray over him, anointing him with oil in the name of the Lord: And the prayer of faith shall save the sick, and the Lord shall raise him up; and if he have committed sins, they shall be forgiven him" (James 5:14,15).

8. *When You Pray The Will Of God, Confidence And Faith Come Easily.* This is important. Your faith is *necessary* for *His* response. "And this is the confidence that we have in Him, that, if we ask any thing according to His will, He heareth us: and if we know that He hear us, whatsoever we ask, we know that we have the petitions that we desired of Him" (1 John 5:14,15).

Your Assignment requires *God.*

Your Assignment requires people, *intercessors.*

Your intercessors greatly influence *the flow of*

favor in your life.

When you truly respect intercession, you will see the most dramatic results you have ever experienced in your lifetime.

⁓ 26 ⁓

SOMEONE IS ALWAYS OBSERVING YOU WHO IS CAPABLE OF GREATLY BLESSING YOU IN YOUR ASSIGNMENT.

⟞⟝

Your struggles and efforts are being noted.

Someone is carefully evaluating your progress, pursuits, and potential. You may not know the person. Perhaps you have not met him or her yet. It would astound you if you knew who are presently discussing your Assignment with great *favor* and appreciation.

This is very important. Your *consistency* is attracting attention. Your ability to stay *focused* is like a magnet. Somebody observing you now is considering entering your life with favor, influence, and support. You will have access to their skills, Wisdom, and circle of friendships...soon. "Seest thou a man diligent in his business? he shall stand before kings; he shall not stand before mean men" (Proverbs 22:29).

People are *asking* about you. Your *endurance* is being admired. Your *integrity* is being mentioned in circles that would thrill and excite you. When these people enter your life, *you will achieve in a single day what would normally require a year for you to accomplish alone.*

Someone is carefully observing your productivity and attitude toward your present boss and superior.

It happened to Ruth. As you will recall, she was the Moabitess who gleaned in the fields of Boaz. She had followed her mother-in-law, Naomi, from Moab back to Bethlehem. Her father-in-law was dead. Her brother-in-law was dead. Her own husband was dead. She did not have any children. She was a lonely, focused, and loyal peasant woman trying to find enough food to survive.

Someone noticed her. Boaz, the wealthy landowner, came to review the Harvest. He looked and saw Ruth. He said to his supervisor of reapers, "Whose damsel is this?" The wealthy study genealogies.

"It is the Moabitish damsel that came back with Naomi out of the country of Moab: And she said, I pray you, let me glean and gather after the reapers among the sheaves: so she came, and hath continued even from the morning until now, that she tarried a little in the house" (Ruth 2:6,7).

Boaz approached Ruth. He explained that protection would be provided as long as she wanted to reap in his field. Her humility and sweet spirit had touched Boaz. Then Boaz explained that he knew who she was and who Naomi was. He confirmed that conversations had taken place concerning her life. "It hath fully been shewed me, all that thou hast done unto thy mother in law since the death of thine husband: and how thou hast left thy father and thy

mother, and the land of thy nativity, and art come unto
a people which thou knewest not heretofore" (Ruth
2:11).
Boldness is a quality every champion admires.
Oh, please listen to me today! You have no idea
how many people are being stirred toward your life
with great *favor*. Every good *Seed* that you have sown
is going to grow and bear fruit. Every *hour* you have
invested in restoring and healing others will produce
an inevitable Harvest! *Your sacrifices are not in vain*.
Your toils and struggles have been noted, *documented*,
and observed by the Lord of the Harvest! "And let us
not be weary in well doing: for in due season we shall
reap, if we faint not" (Galatians 6:9).
The scenario then unfolds as Boaz invites Ruth
to join his servants at meal time. She is permitted to
sit beside the reapers. Boaz instructs his employees
to leave extra barley for her. You see, the rich were
instructed to leave the *corners* of their field for the
poor and strangers to gather food for their own
survival. (See Leviticus 19:9,10.)
But here, Boaz has made a decision to leave
plenty of barley accessible for her. The Bible calls it,
"handfuls of purpose" for her.
You see, this kind of favor always occurs in the
lives of those who are obsessed with their Assignment.
God goes before you. He puts inside the hearts of others
a desire to aid you, *assist you*, and enable you to
complete your Assignment. He is a just God. "The just
Lord is in the midst thereof; He will not do iniquity:
every morning doth He bring His judgment to light,
He faileth not" (Zephaniah 3:5).
So, *someone is always evaluating the way you*

solve problems.

One of the intriguing stories in the Bible is that concerning Rebecca. She was the young virgin daughter of Bethuel. She had gone to the well to fill her pitcher with water.

Meanwhile, the master servant of wealthy Abraham had been assigned to find a wife for Isaac, the son of Abraham. He had prayed concerning her. He had asked God to confirm the bride who, with Isaac, would inherit the incredible wealth of Abraham. His request was unusual. It was rather demanding. He wanted whoever this woman would be to voluntarily offer to water all his camels which had come on the long journey with him.

Imagine this! Imagine the incredible and huge task of replenishing a caravan of camels with a pitcher of water! He wanted a *diligent* woman, an *observant* woman, a *caring* woman. She could not be lazy in the slightest degree if she would be linked to Abraham and Isaac. *They were achievers.*

Wealthy men do not tolerate what poor men will.

It happened. "And when she had done giving him drink, she said, I will draw water for thy camels also, until they have done drinking. And she hasted, and emptied her pitcher into the trough, and ran again unto the well to draw water, and drew for all his camels" (Genesis 24:19,20).

Uncommon women do uncommon things.

She put her own plans aside for that day when she saw a tired and weary traveler.

She did not want the man to take care of her.

She *wanted to take care of the man.*

She did not desire to be served.

She desired to serve.
She did not want someone to make her life easier.
She wanted to make life easier *for someone else.*
She did not wait to be *asked.*
She asked.
She honored the request of the tired man. She did it *speedily.* She had diligence. The Bible said that she hasted, "and ran again unto the well to draw water." She was thorough and "drew for all his camels" (Genesis 24:20).

Servants *notice* servants.

Quality servants discern *quality* serving.

Uncommon servants discern *uncommon* service.

This man was the choice servant of Abraham, one of the wealthiest men in the region. He was trustworthy. Diligent. Caring. His integrity qualified him to select the woman who would inherit the entire wealth of Abraham and Isaac.

Then he asked about her family. He asked if it was possible to lodge there for the night. Her hospitality flowed from her like a river. "She said moreover unto him, We have both straw and provender enough, and room to lodge in" (Genesis 24:25).

Great people are always kind people.

The rest is history. She was chosen, and she married Isaac. She became the mother of Jacob and the grandmother of Joseph. Now you understand where Joseph received his remarkable diligence and ability to care for the affairs of others.

Somebody is carefully observing your reactions to adversity and difficulty. It happened in the life of Paul. He was shipwrecked on the island of Melita. Paul had gathered a bundle of sticks and laid them on the fire. A snake came out of the fire and fastened onto his hand. The barbarians of the island talked among themselves. They thought, "No doubt this man is a murderer, whom, though he hath escaped the sea, yet vengeance suffereth not to live" (Acts 28:4).

But Paul shook off the snake into the fire and felt no harm. *That anointing for conquering affected them.* They changed their minds and "said that he was a god!" (See Acts 28:6.)

Overcoming talks. As others around you observe your life, they will be affected by your focus, victories, and endurance.

Investors study young couples. They observe their aggressiveness and pursuit of excellence before investing. Leaders scrutinize and carefully note the behavior of the assistants of fellow leaders. Every powerful man longs for someone he can trust to work beside him daily. Every aggressive leader searches continually for others who are aggressive, energized, and diligent.

I read my mail carefully. When I see a young minister expanding, pursuing, and emptying his life into his Assignment, it matters to me. When I sow a Seed into his ministry, I am eager to observe the quality of his response back to me.

Put excellence into your present. Do not wait for a glorious future to arrive. *Empty your best into your present. Your* present efforts are being multiplied, noticed, and observed. Rewards are inevitable.

Picture this: You are running daily on the track of life. The grandstands of spectators are observing you—*far more than you could possibly know.* "Wherefore seeing we also are compassed about with so great a cloud of witnesses, let us lay aside every weight, and the sin which doth so easily beset us, and let us run with patience the race that is set before us" (Hebrews 12:1).

Run today with excellence.

Someone is watching who may be the Golden Bridge to your next season.

❦ 27 ❦

YOUR ASSIGNMENT MAY REQUIRE UNUSUAL AND UNWAVERING TRUST IN A MAN OR WOMAN OF GOD.

You will have to trust somebody.

It is true that you cannot trust everyone. You certainly cannot trust everyone every day of your life. But when God determines to bless you, *He will place someone close to you* with an instruction, an encouragement, or a warning that will greatly *influence* your life. Your ability to *trust* their word from God *for you* can be the difference between remarkable success and total failure.

The person you are trusting is deciding your future.

Let me explain. God uses the chain of authority continually in your life. That is why the Apostle Paul encouraged children to obey their parents, employees to honor their boss, and Christians to honor the man of God in their lives.

One of the most powerful principles, hidden like a nugget of gold, is, "Believe in the Lord your God, so shall ye be established; believe His prophets, so shall ye prosper" (2 Chronicles 20:20).

Doubt is costly. Skepticism creates the greatest losses on earth. Unbelief creates disasters as quickly as faith produces miracles. Millions of sinners have forfeited an incredible life in Christ because they *refused to trust* in the words of a man of God. To many, the preaching of the Gospel is foolishness. "For the preaching of the cross is to them that perish foolishness; but unto us which are saved it is the power of God...it pleased God by the foolishness   of preaching to save them that believe"   (1 Corinthians 1:18,21).

God often packages His gold in burlap bags.

You see, the man that God chooses to use may not be intellectual, articulate, or skilled. He may be naive, uneducated, and even uncouth. John the Baptist was certainly not pleasing in appearance by modern standards. But those who embraced his word from God were ushered into new levels of power and *changed forever.*

The Apostle Paul did not impress everyone. He wrote to the church at Corinth, "And I, brethren, when I came to you, came not with excellency of speech or of Wisdom, declaring unto you the testimony of God. And I was with you in weakness, and in fear, and in much trembling. And my speech and my preaching was not with enticing words of man's Wisdom, but in demonstration of the Spirit and of power: That your faith should not stand in the Wisdom of men, but in the   power   of   God" (1 Corinthians 2:1,3-5).

Your financial breakthrough may depend on your willingness to believe a man of God. Your financial provision may require total obedience to an instruction from a man of God. It happened to the widow of Zarephath. She was emaciated and broken. Her son was starving. She was down to her last meal. Elijah, the prophet, knocked on the door of her home with a bold and almost incredulous instruction. The instruction? Give him a meal before even her son ate. *You see, the instruction of a man of God will rarely be logical.* You can do the logical thing without a man of God in your life. But you will rarely do an illogical act unless a man of God *stirs your faith.* Somewhere, at some time, you will need a man of God to move you from the pit of logic to the palace of faith. Elijah did it. "And Elijah said unto her, Fear not; go and do as thou hast said: but make me thereof a little cake first, and bring it unto me, and after make for thee and for thy son. For thus saith the Lord God of Israel, The barrel of meal shall not waste, neither shall the cruse of oil fail, until the day that the Lord sendeth rain upon the earth" (1 Kings 17:13,14).

Your reaction to a man of God determines God's reaction to you.

This is so important: When a man of God gives you an instruction, there is a judgment or a reward that your obedience will produce.

He is not giving an instruction to you to demonstrate his authority.

He is not giving you an instruction to finance his own life.

His instruction is an *exit* from your present crisis.

His instruction is an *entry* to a miracle Harvest.

Your obedience will determine your own reward.

The widow obeyed. *The Golden Key to success is always Obedience to an instruction from God.* "And she went and did according to the saying of Elijah: and she, and he, and her house, did eat many days. And the barrel of meal wasted not, neither did the cruse of oil fail, according to the word of the Lord, *which He spake by Elijah*" (1 Kings 17:15,16). [Emphasis added.]

Read 1 Kings 17 carefully. You will not find a single reference proving the widow recognized or heard the voice of God directly. The prophet heard God. She heard the prophet.

God spoke to the prophet.

The *prophet* spoke to the *widow*.

That sequence is honored by God.

When man refuses to accept an instruction *through someone God sends*, he loses *every promise* and reward God had intended.

When God wants to bless you, He will talk to a man of God about your life. When God wants to stop judgment, He usually sends a man of God *with a warning.* He did it to Nineveh. "Now the word of the Lord came unto Jonah the son of Amittai, saying, Arise, go to Nineveh, that great city, and cry against it; for their wickedness is come up before Me" (Jonah 1:1,2).

Now Jonah was disobedient. His experience in "Seaweed University" is known around the world. He was swallowed up by a fish, and his own disobedience was costly. So when he arrived in Nineveh, he was a *persuaded* man.

Persuaded men persuade.

Let me say this: Thousands of people have no idea what a man of God experiences prior to giving an instruction to someone. There have been many nights in my life when an instruction came from the Lord for people and I really did not want to give it. It was not always encouraging. I have been given judgment instructions more than once. But the reason I obeyed was not to secure the approval, applause, and acceptance of people. Rather, I had a powerful God speaking powerfully and persuasively into my ear. *My disobedience* would be too costly.

Jonah cried in the streets of Nineveh, "Yet forty days, and Nineveh shall be overthrown" (Jonah 3:4).

Somehow, the credibility and truth of his message was felt. The people were repentant. "So the people of Nineveh believed God, and proclaimed a fast, and put on sackcloth, from the greatest of them even to the least of them. For word came unto the king of Nineveh, and he arose from his throne, and he laid his robe from him, and covered him with sackcloth, and sat in ashes. And he caused it to be proclaimed and published through Nineveh by the decree of the king and his nobles, saying, Let neither man nor beast, herd nor flock, taste any thing: let them not feed, nor drink water: But let man and beast be covered with sackcloth, and cry mightily unto God: yea, let them turn every one from his evil way, and from the violence that is in their hands. Who can tell if God will turn and repent, and turn away from His fierce anger, that we perish not?" (Jonah 3:5-9).

Think about this: The king wept and cried. The people were instructed to stop feeding their animals and flocks. The animals themselves were forced to fast. The senators and government leaders went without food.

Something supernatural happens when you decide to believe a man of God.

What was their reward for trusting the word of a man of God? "And God saw their works, that they turned from their evil way; and God repented of the evil, that He had said that He would do unto them; and *He did it not*" (Jonah 3:10). [Emphasis added.]

I had a very unusual experience that changed my life. Each year I host a World Wisdom Conference. It happened two years ago during a service at my World Wisdom Conference. One of my friends, a visiting evangelist came to me saying, "I feel that God spoke to me to receive an offering for your ministry today."

"Well, I will let you know whatever God impresses me to do," I replied. I appreciated what he said. But, I really felt that I was able to hear from God as much as anyone else present. I felt no leading whatsoever that an offering was to be received at that time.

A few minutes later, another evangelist handed me a note. It reiterated that the other brother felt impressed to receive an offering. They both felt it was God and wanted me to hand him the microphone. I was agitated.

I had a personal schedule for the time that offerings would be received. My basic attitude was, "This is my own conference. Nobody is going to receive an offering unless I approve and *know* that it is the will of God. This is neither the time nor the place for an offering." I had already received an offering that morning, and I did not want the people to feel harassed.

I am not a novice in the ministry. I have walked to the pulpit more than 12,000 times since I started preaching at the age of eight years old. I spoke at my first crusade at the age of 15. I entered full-time evangelism at the age of 19. I have been in 36 countries of the world. I was a little peeved that another man of God would push me in this manner.

Now, while I was speaking and preparing to dismiss the people for lunch, this evangelist walked up to me publicly. He was weeping and crying. "Brother, could I say a word?" I was still frustrated. It bothered me deeply. I pray, fast, and make every effort to hear the voice of the Holy Spirit. *I was hearing nothing from God.* I *felt* nothing. Somehow, I really believed in my heart that he was totally out of order.

But, he was a man of God. I *knew* that he was a man of God. His ministry was *proven.* His anointing was *obvious.* He had passed the test of time. He wore the badge of *endurance.* He was gentle and kind, but very persistent. So I handed him the microphone, very reluctantly.

As he began to speak, tears ran down his cheeks. Within moments my partners began to step out of their seats streaming to the front with $1,000 faith promises for the ministry. They kept coming, and coming, and coming. I stood there, *still feeling nothing.* I could hardly believe what was happening. I cannot say that I felt joy, because I did not feel joy. I never did feel a confirmation. During the entire time that he received the offering, I *never* felt the winds of the Holy Spirit. The offering that day in cash and pledges was more than $100,000.

I prayed, "Oh Lord, I thought I knew Your voice. I thought I knew when You spoke."

You see, *God had spoken to another man something He had withheld from me.* It concerned me deeply. I was incensed. I was embarrassed. I was puzzled. I am sure that was the way Eli the priest felt when God spoke to Samuel, the little boy, instead of him, the high priest. I felt the timing was wrong. I had my own schedule. *The only reason* I had finally allowed and permitted him to do what he did was because *I really knew* he was a man of God. The touch of God was upon him. I *felt* nothing. I *saw* no vision. I *experienced* no revelation. *I simply trusted in the man of God* that my Father had decided to use that day.

I learned that *God tells others things He will not tell me.* It continues to irritate me, but I learned a valuable lesson.

My success will depend on my ability to recognize a man of God when I am in his presence.

Once, I was ministering on the East Coast. A remarkable anointing came upon me, and I shared a personal testimony regarding planting Seeds of $58. Let me explain. Six years ago I was sitting on the platform in Washington, D.C. The pastor was receiving the tithes and offerings. I had been sowing a Seed of $1,000 each month into that church for the previous twelve months.

While the pastor was receiving the tithes, the Holy Spirit suddenly spoke to me. He asked a question. "How many kinds of blessings are in my Word?"

Well, I had done a private study. In my research, I had found 58 different kinds of blessings. Now, there may be more depending on your own selection of categories, but that is what I counted. So I replied, "There are 58 different kinds of blessings in your Word."

"I want you to plant a special Seed of $58 in this

offering. Write 'Covenant of Blessing' on the check." He told me that He wanted this Seed of $58 to represent a covenant of blessing between Him and me. I thought it was ridiculous. But as I listened from my heart, I knew His voice. I obeyed. A few moments later, He instructed me to plant another Seed for someone I loved who needed a miracle in their life. I obeyed. Within weeks, miracles occurred in my life that were explosive and life-changing.

So in the Sunday morning service, I shared my experience. I explained to the people that I felt strongly impressed that each person present in the service should sow a Seed of $58 toward the work of the Lord. It would be used to purchase television air time to teach the Gospel. Many people obeyed that instruction—not because they heard the voice of God, but because *they believed* that a man of God was giving them an appropriate and godly instruction.

That afternoon, one of the men visiting the church called the pastor. He was irate. He was an ungodly man who did not follow the Lord. He told the pastor that the whole thing was a scheme, a hoax, a trap. You see, *when you do not know God, it is obvious that you will not necessarily recognize a man of God.* When you live in daily disobedience, it is normal to continue that disobedience when an instruction comes from God.

In that service another visiting pastor took her checkbook and planted a Seed of $58. She believed that the mantle of favor would be wrapped around her life *because she obeyed an instruction* I had given.

Within a few months, an elderly man she had attended to died. When he died, he left this lady pastor a church paid for in full, two homes, and 27 acres of land. The blessings of God exploded in her life. *She had obeyed the instructions of a man of God.* They were not logical. They were beyond human comprehension. She did not "buy a miracle." She had *obeyed an instruction.*

The man who criticized...*lost* his Harvest.

The woman who obeyed...*created* a Harvest.

Two people in the same service produced two different results. Oh, please hear me today! When God wants to bless you, He will anoint a wonderful man or woman of God to give you an instruction. It may be illogical. It may be ridiculous. But, remember Naaman? He had leprosy. He was the captain of the host of the armies of Syria. Yet when he willingly obeyed the instruction of a prophet to dip in the Jordan River seven times, *his leprosy disappeared.*

It will happen the same way *in your life.* When you know someone is truly a man or woman of God, *be swift to embrace their instruction.*

Your destiny is your decision.

❧ 28 ❧

THE PROBLEM THAT INFURIATES YOU THE MOST IS OFTEN THE PROBLEM GOD HAS ASSIGNED YOU TO SOLVE.

Anger is a clue to your anointing and Assignment.
When Moses saw an Egyptian beating an Israelite, anger rose up within him. That anger was a *clue*. It was a *signal*. The situation that infuriated him was the one God had ordained him to change, correct, and alter.

Anger is the birthplace of change. Situations only change when anger is born. You will not solve a problem, consciously or unconsciously, until you experience a holy and righteous anger rising up within you.

You will not change a situation until it becomes intolerable.

For many years in the South, African-Americans were forced by law to sit in the back of the bus. They might still be doing that today had it not been for a courageous woman named Rosa Parks. This work-weary black lady took her place in the back of a crowded bus in Montgomery, Alabama. When the bus filled, she refused to stand for a white man to have her seat. It was the catalyst for dramatic, appropriate, and long-needed change in America. That kind of courage deserves honor and respect. *Whatever you can tolerate, you cannot change.* Whatever you refuse to accept, whatever makes you mad enough to take action, is a clue to your Assignment.

MADD, Mothers Against Drunk Driving, was started by a mother who saw her child killed on the street by a drunken driver. Her anger birthed a response. *You must become mad about the present before the future will listen to you.*

If you can adapt to your present, you will never enter your future. Only those who cannot tolerate the present are qualified to enter their future.

It has happened in my own life. When I was a teenager, I felt a great attraction to the courtroom. I wanted to be an attorney. I sat for hours in those courtrooms in my little hometown of Lake Charles, Louisiana. I took notes by the hour on cases that came up. I still have a hatred of injustice.

I can become angry about it right now while I am writing you this chapter, just thinking about people who have not been represented properly. I read law books continually and still continually read books dealing with the legal system. Watching the process of law and observing the manipulation that occurs in the courtroom still infuriates me. I believe this *anger is a clue to the anointing on my life.*

Ignorance angers me. When I talk to people who

are uninformed, something comes alive in me. A desire to teach is overwhelming. I speak at seminars throughout the world. Sometimes I almost miss my airplane schedule because I become so obsessed with teaching that to walk out of the seminar becomes extremely difficult.

Unproductive employees are a source of great agitation to me. I believe it is a clue to a mantle on my life. It is important to me that I unlock the mystery of achievement through Wisdom Keys and books that I write.

Listen carefully to ministers who teach about prosperity. *They hate poverty.* They despise lack. It grieves them deeply to see families wounded, destroyed, and devastated because of poverty. Their messages are full of fury and sound almost angry! Why? Destroying poverty is a calling *within* them.

Have you ever listened to ministers who have an anointing for deliverance? They become angry toward demonic spirits that possess family members.

Listen to a soul-winning evangelist. Do you hear his passion? He is moved with compassion when he sees the unsaved and those who are uncommitted to Christ.

Anger reveals an anointing. "And it shall come to pass in that day, that his burden shall be taken away from off thy shoulder, and His yoke from off thy neck, and the yoke shall be destroyed *because of the anointing*" (Isaiah 10:27). [Emphasis added.] The anointing is the *burden-removing, yoke-destroying power of God in your life.*

So, pay attention to whatever angers you. Something inside you rises up strongly against it.

Why? *Your anger qualifies you to be an enemy of that problem.* God is preparing *you* to *solve* it.

Anger is *energy.*

Anger is *power.*

Anger *moves hell.*

Anger can *master a situation.*

Unfocused, anger destroys and ruins.

Focused properly, it creates miraculous change.

Anger merely requires proper focus. Develop it. You must see your anger as an instruction from God to stay in The Secret Place to *find the solution for the problem*, obtain the weapons to destroy the enemy, and *develop a daily agenda* designed by the Holy Spirit...*to create change.*

Angry people can dramatically change their generation.

≈ 29 ≈

WHAT YOU LOVE MOST IS A CLUE TO YOUR ASSIGNMENT.

Passion is magnetic.

What do you *love to discuss*? What do you love to *hear about*? What *excites* you? These are clues to your Assignment. These are clues to your abilities.

You will always have Wisdom toward whatever you love.

If you love children, you will probably possess an innate and obvious Wisdom toward *children*.

If you love computers, you will discover a natural inclination to understand this *computer age*.

If you love to work on cars, you will have a natural Wisdom toward *mechanical things*.

Great singers do not normally say, "I really hate singing. I would rather sell cars. God is making me sing." Of course not. They *love* to sing.

Have you ever heard an extraordinary man of God say, "I secretly dream of raising worms!" Of course not. You will never hear a great pianist say, "I hate playing the piano. It is something *I have* to do. God is *making* me do it. I would much rather be building houses."

You see, *what you love is a clue to your Assignment.*

When God calls you to an Assignment, obey Him. Within due time He will also birth an inner desire for that specific Assignment. It is His way of honoring your obedience. Yet some of us were taught the opposite. I remember one of the ladies in my father's church saying, "If God calls you to preach the Gospel overseas and you refuse, He will make you go, just like He did with Jonah! If you tell God you do not want to do something, He will make you do it."

God gave Jonah an instruction to go to Nineveh. He chose to go to Tarshish. Note this: Why did he not simply stay where he was? He did not have to leave where he was. *Something within him was moving him.* He simply refused to complete the Assignment.

His Assignment was twofold: 1) Leave where he was, and 2) Arrive in Nineveh. He *started* his Assignment. God dealt with him for his rebellion in not completing his Assignment.

God is not looking for new ways to antagonize you, agitate you, and make you miserable. When He calls you to do something, if you will remain in His presence and stay obedient, He will eventually give you a *desire to complete it.*

What *really* excites you? What brings *great enthusiasm?* What are you doing on the *happiest days* of your life?

Those desires are signposts toward your place of Assignment.

⧼ 30 ⧽

YOUR ASSIGNMENT MAY SEEM SMALL, YET BE THE GOLDEN LINK IN A GREAT CHAIN OF MIRACLES.

Acorns create oak trees.

There is an interesting story in the Old Testament. A great general, Naaman, had leprosy. The servant girl in the house *told her mistress* that there was a prophet in Israel who could cure her master if he would go to the prophet and ask for help. Naaman went, heard the instruction to dip in the Jordan River seven times and *came back healed of his leprosy.*

That little servant girl created one of the greatest miracles of the Old Testament. The story of obeying the prophet's illogical instruction—to dip in the Jordan River—has been told countless times by thousands of ministers. It has unleashed waves of faith and created a collection of miracles known only by God.

Yet, she was just one servant girl.

She simply recommended a man of God.

Philip, the preaching deacon, was suddenly translated from the heat of a revival in Jerusalem to the chariot of an Ethiopian eunuch traveling through the desert. Historians tell us that one conversation

Philip had with the eunuch caused 90 percent of Ethiopia to become converted to Christianity.

Yet, he was just one deacon talking to one man in a chariot.

Years ago, a man lay dying on his death bed in Fort Worth, Texas. His sister up north sent him a letter urging him to go to a local healing revival. His friends took him there the next night. That night he was gloriously converted to Christ. The second night he was healed instantly and called into the ministry. That man became one of the greatest preachers in decades, and it is said that he brought more than one million people to Christ through his crusade ministry.

Yet, it was just one simple letter from a sister a thousand miles away.

Small insignificant actions often set in motion the greatest forces on earth. Never minimize *anything.* Nothing is little to the Creator. "For who hath despised the day of small things?" (Zechariah 4:10). "Though thy beginning was small, yet thy latter end should greatly increase" (Job 8:7).

The little boy had five loaves and two fishes. The crowd waited. Jesus took his five loaves and two fishes and began to break them up to feed the people. The rest is history. That miracle of multiplication has been heralded around the world. Countless miracles have occurred because of people just like you and me embracing this great miracle.

One little boy. Five loaves and two fishes.

An amazing miracle of multiplication.

Your Assignment may seem small at times. Do not worry about it. Do not focus on that aspect. I am sure Miriam remembered placing her infant brother in the muddy waters of the river Nile. Who could foresee that the daughter of Pharaoh would take him for her own son? Who would have known that from that little basket would come the world's greatest deliverer of the *entire Hebrew nation?*

Every small thing really does matter.

Acorns are simply the beginning of oak trees.

Satan fears your future far more than your present. Do not be discouraged or feel insignificant. You are setting in motion waves of blessing that will destroy the deserts of pain for many.

Nothing Is Little In The Hands Of A Multiplier.

∾ 31 ∾

YOU ARE THE ONLY ONE GOD HAS ANOINTED FOR YOUR SPECIFIC ASSIGNMENT.

Your Assignment requires your participation.

Nobody else can *discern* it for you. Nobody else can *pursue it* for you. Nobody else can *complete* it for you. "So then every one of us shall give account of himself to God" (Romans 14:12).

It is sad to listen to those who blame their circumstances on others. I have often listened to a husband whine, "I want to do it, but my wife does not agree with me." Wives often complain, "My husband will not cooperate with my calling and Assignment."

Stop blaming others for your personal decisions. One of the most important principles spoken into my life by the Holy Spirit has been the Wisdom Key, "Never complain about what you permit."

Never complain about what you permit.

Your present circumstances are existing *with your permission.* Your toleration of them breathes life and longevity into them. *Intolerance* of your present will create a *different* future. *Nothing will really change in your life until you cannot tolerate the present any longer.*

The apostle Paul was very direct: "But let every

man prove his own work, and then shall he have *rejoicing in himself alone*, and not in another" (Galatians 6:4). [Emphasis added.] You see, God never intended for you to depend on everyone else for the completion of your Assignment. Your real joy depends on *His presence*. His presence depends on your pursuit. *Your pursuit* is *your own decision.*

Certainly, hindrances occur. It is common to have relationships that slow us down, demotivate us and discourage us. Every achiever has experienced a connection with someone who was a burden instead of a blessing. But *you* have chosen your friendships! *The quality of your relationships reflects and reveals what you respect the most in life.* When I read the biographies of extraordinary champions, they continually take personal responsibility for their own actions, decisions, and the tasks necessary to reach their goals and dreams.

"I really hate my job," one man confessed to me.

"Then, why are you staying there?" I asked, quite puzzled.

"It is close to my house," was his ridiculous reply. *You have chosen the present.* You can leave it or change it.

You may complain, whine, and gripe for the rest of your life. But you have chosen *the environment* surrounding you. You have *accepted* it. You have *embraced* it. You have *refused to walk away from it.* So stop finding fault with it.

Your present exists with your permission.

The Apostle Paul took a personal responsibility for his life. At the close of his life, he wrote Timothy, "I have fought a good fight, I have finished my course, I have kept the faith" (2 Timothy 4:7). Nobody else fought his fight. Nobody else could finish his course for him. Nobody else could run his race. He kept his faith. He kept his own focus. He fought his own fight. *You must grasp this.* You must decide the *conclusion* of your life that you desire. You must decide to *run your own race. You* must grow the kind of Harvest *you* desire. You must pursue the relationships that matter to you, not to others. The Apostle Paul had a glimpse of this principle. "Wherefore, my beloved, as ye have always obeyed, not as in my presence only, but now much more in my absence, *work out your own salvation* with fear and trembling" (Philippians 2:12). *That is why your complaining must stop.* You are responsible for your situations. "Do all things without murmurings and disputings," encouraged Paul. (See Philippians 2:14.)

Jesus, our example and pattern, declared, "I have finished the work which Thou gavest Me to do" (John 17:4). He took responsibility for His own Assignment.

You may be deeply disturbed and uncomfortable with your life right now.

Here Are Four Keys That Can Move You From Discomfort Into The Proper Season Of Your Assignment:

1. *Ask Yourself Probing, Sincere, And Direct Questions.* Have you exhausted the benefits of your present season? Have you extracted from your boss or mentors everything they have wanted to pour into you? Does your present schedule reveal that you have

honored your priorities *in the eyes of God*? Have you excelled and given your *very best* to those you are laboring among *at this time*?

You see, if you have *not* emptied and maximized your life into the *present*, you are *unqualified* to enter your future. *Your future is a reward, not a guarantee.* That is why the Apostle Paul made this statement after discussing the quality of his fight and the finishing of his course. "Henceforth there is laid up for me a crown of righteousness, which the Lord, the righteous judge, shall give me at that day: and not to me only, but unto all them also that love his appearing" (2 Timothy 4:8).

2. *Have You Spent Enough Time In His Presence To Hear The Voice Of The Holy Spirit*? You see, He is your Mentor and Advisor. If He is not speaking into your life daily and observing your continual acts of obedience, nothing in your life could possibly be accurate. Consequently, your assessments of your life may be distorted and inaccurate.

3. *Are You Living In Rebellion To Any Known Law Of God?* I have found that it is impossible to experience total peace when one moment of my daily life is lived in opposition to His laws. "And whatsoever we ask, we receive of Him, because we keep His commandments, and do those things that are pleasing in His sight" (1 John 3:22).

4. *Is The Future I Am Desiring Worth My Seed Of Patience And The Investment Of Preparation?* Moses wanted to be the deliverer for Israel. But he had to endure seasons of preparation. Jesus had thirty years of preparation before His public ministry. Sometimes in my own life, I have desired deeply a different future, but I was unwilling to pay the price

of preparation for it.

Your Assignment is something you *do*, not something you observe. Read the writings of the Apostle Paul. "...I *follow* after...I *do*...I *press*...I *beseech*...I *entreat* thee" (Philippians 3:12-4:3). Your Assignment is action. Achievement. Activity. Movement. Productivity. Accomplishment. Energy.

Thank you for giving me access to your life. It is not an accident that these burning Wisdom Keys have now passed from my heart into your heart.

God has connected us, my precious friend.

Now, go and succeed with your Assignment... Beyond Anything You Have Ever Dreamed Before.

ORDER FORM THE MIKE MURDOCK WISDOM LIBRARY
(All books paperback unless indicated otherwise.)

Qty	Code	Book Title	USA	Total
	B01	WISDOM FOR WINNING	$10	
	B02	5 STEPS OUT OF DEPRESSION	$ 3	
	B03	THE SEX TRAP	$ 3	
	B04	10 LIES PEOPLE BELIEVE ABOUT MONEY	$ 3	
	B05	FINDING YOUR PURPOSE IN LIFE	$ 3	
	B06	CREATING TOMORROW THROUGH SEED-FAITH	$ 3	
	B07	BATTLE TECHNIQUES FOR WAR WEARY SAINTS	$ 3	
	B08	ENJOYING THE WINNING LIFE	$ 3	
	B09	FOUR FORCES/GUARANTEE CAREER SUCCESS	$ 3	
	B10	THE BRIDGE CALLED DIVORCE	$ 3	
	B11	DREAM SEEDS	$ 9	
	B12	YOUNG MINISTERS HANDBOOK	$20	
	B13	SEEDS OF WISDOM ON DREAMS AND GOALS	$ 3	
	B14	SEEDS OF WISDOM ON RELATIONSHIPS	$ 3	
	B15	SEEDS OF WISDOM ON MIRACLES	$ 3	
	B16	SEEDS OF WISDOM ON SEED-FAITH	$ 3	
	B17	SEEDS OF WISDOM ON OVERCOMING	$ 3	
	B18	SEEDS OF WISDOM ON HABITS	$ 3	
	B19	SEEDS OF WISDOM ON WARFARE	$ 3	
	B20	SEEDS OF WISDOM ON OBEDIENCE	$ 3	
	B21	SEEDS OF WISDOM ON ADVERSITY	$ 3	
	B22	SEEDS OF WISDOM ON PROSPERITY	$ 3	
	B23	SEEDS OF WISDOM ON PRAYER	$ 3	
	B24	SEEDS OF WISDOM ON FAITH-TALK	$ 3	
	B25	SEEDS OF WISDOM ONE YEAR DEVOTIONAL	$10	
	B26	THE GOD BOOK	$10	
	B27	THE JESUS BOOK	$10	
	B28	THE BLESSING BIBLE	$10	
	B29	THE SURVIVAL BIBLE	$10	
	B30	THE TEEN'S TOPICAL BIBLE	$ 6	
	B30L	THE TEEN'S TOPICAL BIBLE (LEATHER)	$20	
	B31	THE ONE-MINUTE TOPICAL BIBLE	$10	
	B32	THE MINISTER'S TOPICAL BIBLE	$ 6	
	B33	THE BUSINESSMAN'S TOPICAL BIBLE	$ 6	
	B33L	THE BUSINESSMAN'S TOPICAL BIBLE (LEATHER)	$20	
	B34L	THE GRANDPARENT'S TOPICAL BIBLE (LEATHER)	$20	
	B35	THE FATHER'S TOPICAL BIBLE	$ 6	
	B35L	THE FATHER'S TOPICAL BIBLE (LEATHER)	$20	
	B36	THE MOTHER'S TOPICAL BIBLE	$ 6	
	B36L	THE MOTHER'S TOPICAL BIBLE (LEATHER)	$20	
	B37	THE NEW CONVERT'S TOPICAL BIBLE	$15	
	B38	THE WIDOW'S TOPICAL BIBLE	$ 6	
	B39	THE DOUBLE DIAMOND PRINCIPLE	$ 9	
	B40	WISDOM FOR CRISIS TIMES	$ 9	
	B41	THE GIFT OF WISDOM (VOLUME ONE)	$ 8	
	B42	ONE-MINUTE BUSINESSMAN'S DEVOTIONAL	$10	
	B43	ONE-MINUTE BUSINESSWOMAN'S DEVOTIONAL	$10	
	B44	31 SECRETS FOR CAREER SUCCESS	$10	
	B45	101 WISDOM KEYS	$ 7	
	B46	31 FACTS ABOUT WISDOM	$ 7	
	B47	THE COVENANT OF THE FIFTY-EIGHT BLESSINGS	$ 8	
	B48	31 KEYS TO A NEW BEGINNING	$ 7	
	B49	THE PROVERBS 31 WOMAN	$ 7	
	B50	ONE-MINUTE POCKET BIBLE FOR THE ACHIEVER	$ 5	
	B51	ONE-MINUTE POCKET BIBLE FOR FATHERS	$ 5	
	B52	ONE-MINUTE POCKET BIBLE FOR MOTHERS	$ 5	

QTY	CODE	BOOK TITLE	USA	TOTAL
	B53	ONE-MINUTE POCKET BIBLE FOR TEENAGERS	$ 5	
	B54	ONE-MINUTE DEVOTIONAL (HARDBACK)	$14	
	B55	20 KEYS TO A HAPPIER MARRIAGE	$ 3	
	B56	HOW TO TURN MISTAKES INTO MIRACLES	$ 3	
	B57	31 SECRETS OF THE UNFORGETTABLE WOMAN	$ 9	
	B58	MENTOR'S MANNA ON ATTITUDE	$ 3	
	B59	THE MAKING OF A CHAMPION	$ 6	
	B60	ONE-MINUTE POCKET BIBLE FOR MEN	$ 5	
	B61	ONE-MINUTE POCKET BIBLE FOR WOMEN	$ 5	
	B62	ONE-MINUTE POCKET BIBLE/BUS.PROFESSIONALS	$ 5	
	B63	ONE-MINUTE POCKET BIBLE FOR TRUCKERS	$ 5	
	B64	7 OBSTACLES TO ABUNDANT SUCCESS	$ 3	
	B65	BORN TO TASTE THE GRAPES	$ 3	
	B66	GREED, GOLD AND GIVING	$ 3	
	B67	GIFT OF WISDOM FOR CHAMPIONS	$ 8	
	B68	GIFT OF WISDOM FOR ACHIEVERS	$ 8	
	B69	WISDOM KEYS FOR A POWERFUL PRAYER LIFE	$ 3	
	B70	GIFT OF WISDOM FOR MOTHERS	$ 8	
	B71	WISDOM - GOD'S GOLDEN KEY TO SUCCESS	$ 7	
	B72	THE GREATEST SUCCESS HABIT ON EARTH	$ 3	
	B73	THE MENTOR'S MANNA ON ABILITIES	$ 3	
	B74	THE ASSIGNMENT: DREAM/DESTINY #1	$10	
	B75	THE ASSIGNMENT: ANOINTING/ADVERSITY #2	$10	
	B76	THE MENTOR'S MANNA ON THE ASSIGNMENT	$ 3	
	B77	THE GIFT OF WISDOM FOR FATHERS	$ 8	
	B78	THE MENTOR'S MANNA ON THE SECRET PLACE	$ 3	
	B79	THE MENTOR'S MANNA ON ACHIEVEMENT	$ 3	
	B80	THE DOUBLE DIAMOND DAILY DEVOTIONAL	$12	
	B81	THE MENTOR'S MANNA ON ADVERSITY	$ 3	
	B82	31 REASONS PEOPLE DO NOT RECEIVE THEIR FINANCIAL HARVEST	$12	
	B83	THE GIFT OF WISDOM FOR WIVES	$ 8	
	B84	THE GIFT OF WISDOM FOR HUSBANDS	$ 8	
	B85	THE GIFT OF WISDOM FOR TEENAGERS	$ 8	
	B86	THE GIFT OF WISDOM FOR LEADERS	$ 8	
	B87	THE GIFT OF WISDOM FOR GRADUATES	$ 8	
	B88	THE GIFT OF WISDOM FOR BRIDES	$ 8	
	B89	THE GIFT OF WISDOM FOR GROOMS	$ 8	
	B90	THE GIFT OF WISDOM FOR MINISTERS	$ 8	
	B91H	THE LEADERSHIP SECRETS OF JESUS (HDBK)	$15	
	B92	SECRETS OF THE JOURNEY (VOL. 1)	$ 5	
	B93	SECRETS OF THE JOURNEY (VOL. 2)	$ 5	
	B94	SECRETS OF THE JOURNEY (VOL. 3)	$ 5	
	B95	SECRETS OF THE JOURNEY (VOL. 4)	$ 5	

❑ CASH   ❑ CHECK   ❑ MONEY ORDER

❑ CREDIT CARD #   ❑ VISA   ❑ MC   ❑ AMEX

EXPIRATION DATE [　　　　　]   *SORRY NO C.O.D.'s*

SIGNATURE _____

TOTAL PAGE 2	$
TOTAL PAGE 1	$
*ADD SHIPPING 10% USA/20% OTHERS	$
CANADA CURRENCY DIFFERENCE ADD20%	$
TOTAL ENCLOSED	$

PLEASE PRINT

Name [　　　　　　　　　　　　　　　　　]

Address [　　　　　　　　　　　　　　　　　]

City [　　　　　　　　　　　　　　　　　]
State　　Zip

Phone ([　　　]) [　　] - [　　　　]

MIKE MURDOCK

- Began full-time evangelism at the age of 19, which has continued for 34 years.

- Has traveled and spoken to more than 14,000 audiences in 36 countries, including East Africa, the Orient, and Europe.

- Noted author of 115 books, including best sellers, *Wisdom for Winning, Dream Seeds and The Double Diamond Principle.*

- Created the popular *"Wisdom Topical Bible"* series for Businessmen, Mothers, Fathers, Teenagers, and the *One-Minute Pocket Bible.*

- Has composed more than 5,600 songs such as *I Am Blessed, You Can Make It, and Jesus Just The Mention Of Your Name,* recorded by many artists.

- Is the Founder of the Wisdom Center in Dallas, Texas.

- Has a weekly television program called *"Wisdom Keys With Mike Murdock".*

- He has appeared often on TBN, CBN, Oral Roberts and other television network programs.

- Is a Founding Trustee on the Board of International Charismatic Bible Ministries founded by Oral Roberts.

- Has seen over 3,400 accept the call into full-time ministry under his ministry.

- Has embraced his Assignment: *Pursuing... Possessing... And Publishing The Wisdom Of God To Heal The Broken In This Generation.*

THE MINISTRY

1 **Wisdom Books & Literature** -115 best-selling Wisdom books and Teaching tapes that teach the Wisdom of God to thousands.

2 **Church Crusades** - Multitudes are ministered to in crusades and seminars throughout America in "The Uncommon Wisdom Conferences."

3 **Music Ministry** - Millions have been blessed by the anointed songwriting and singing of Mike Murdock, who has written over 5,600 songs.

4 **Television** - "Wisdom Keys With Mike Murdock," a nationally-syndicated weekly television program.

5 **The Wisdom Center** - Where Dr. Murdock holds annual Schools of Ministry for those training for a more excellent ministry.

6 **Schools of the Holy Spirit** - Mike Murdock hosts Schools of the Holy Spirit to mentor believers on the Person and companionship of the Holy Spirit.

7 **Schools of Wisdom** - Each year Mike Murdock hosts Schools of Wisdom for those who want personalized and advanced training for achieving "The Uncommon Dream."

8 **Missionary Ministry** - Dr. Murdock's overseas outreaches to 36 countries have included crusades to East Africa, South America, and Europe.

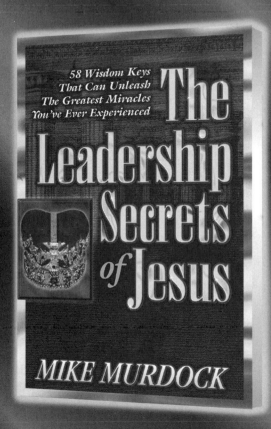

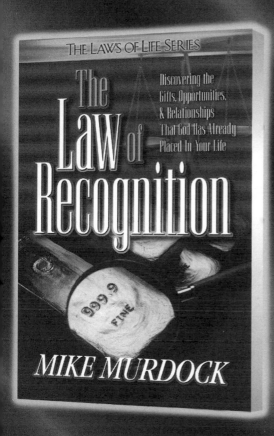

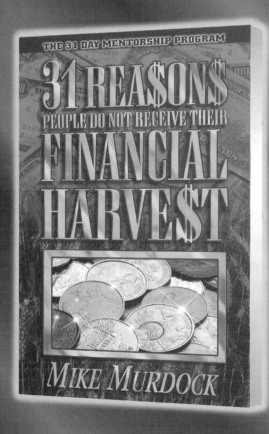

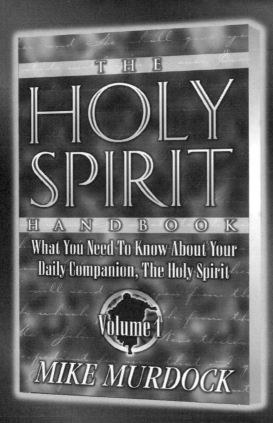